Enjoy chell the world

SHE'S
BACK

D1341354

SHE'S
BACK

YOUR GUIDE TO
RETURNING TO WORK

LISA UNWIN and **DEB KHAN**

Urbane
PUBLICATIONS
urbanepublications.com

First published in Great Britain in 2018 by
Urbane Publications Ltd
Suite 3, Brown Europe House,
33/34 Gleaming Wood Drive, Chatham,
Kent ME5 8RZ
Copyright © Lisa Unwin and Deb Khan, 2018

A CIP catalogue record for this book is available
from the British Library.

ISBN 978-1-911583-56-1
MOBI 978-1-911583-57-8

Design and Typeset by Julie Martin
Cover by Julie Martin

Urbane
PUBLICATIONS

urbanepublications.com

" This is an important book about an issue that could scarcely be more contemporary. The spirit of *She's Back* is the spirit of the age. Read, or be left behind. **"**

MATTHEW D'ANCONA

" A must-have guide to get more women back into the workplace. **"**

ARIANNA HUFFINGTON

" If you're a professional woman who wants to unlock your potential at the same time as raising a family, this book is a must-read. If you're a CEO or business owner who wants to unlock the potential of your whole workforce, this book is for you. And if you care about future-proofing the UK economy at a time of heightened economic uncertainty, this is essential reading. **"**

SARAH WOOD, OBE

Contents

SECTION ONE

Prologue

It's tough out there. Whether you're looking to return to work after a break, changing direction completely, or stepping up again after stepping back, for whatever reason, be under no illusion – it can be a slog.

We are bringing some data to the table. Evidence about what's happening today and information about what you need to do to reignite your career. We use real life stories as inspiration for what's possible, and have gathered hints, tips, strategies and tactics to help you make your return a success.

WHY WOMEN STEP BACK

Women need and want to work. They've trained for it, they're good at it. They like it. Fact. Many women regularly shine at work. But here's the rub: many women also want children. Always have, always will. They may often take on the bulk of caring responsibilities when family members are struck by ill health as well. Turns out they're pretty good at that too.

For thousands of women work and family may not mix. A lack of flexibility at work forces their hand. The prohibitive cost of childcare means work doesn't pay. Too many women are forced to choose. Worse still, when circumstances change, and they are in a position to return, they find their way back blocked.

The result? Talented, well-trained, brilliant women find themselves on the bench, unable to secure well paid, fulfilling and challenging work.

Surely we should have this fixed by now? Not just for women, but for their partners, employers and families. It can be different.

This book nails what's happening now and why. It pinpoints why, despite all the rhetoric and well-meaning initiatives, we still see thousands of women leaving successful careers in their droves. And it outlines a way forward.

It's underpinned by our qualitative and quantitative research, conducted across a range of sectors, which tells the story of thousands of women who feel unable to fulfil their potential.

It's inspired by the words of amazing women who contributed to that research:

> **"**I'm 40 years old; my kids are 10 and 12; I have twenty years to make a discernible impact. Where do I go? What do I do? Who do I talk to? How do I get back in the game?**"**

It's also for younger women who are looking ahead and can't see anyone balancing work and family in a way they aspire to.

Women who want to see that working life doesn't end after kids. It's for the younger women who think this will never happen to them. And it's for anyone – man or woman – who hopes to find both meaning and balance in their working lives.

WHY US?

There's already a wealth of views. Campaigns a-plenty. Non-stop networking. A tsunami of column inches. Endless tomes. All worthy and well-intended; and yet to date a whole stack of talking and writing seems to be leading to a whole heap of nothing.

What are we bringing to this overloaded table?

1. We sought answers to some tough questions

The value of having more women in work has been proven by lots of oft-cited research. What has been missing is the hard core facts, data and numbers around women who drop out. Why do they leave? What do they do? Would they return? Under what circumstances? What would help? What's getting in the way?

It struck us that no one was asking these questions. So we did. Fuelled by a heady mix of fury, pragmatism, chutzpah and a weighty contact book – earned through years of sheer hard graft – off we set. We noticed a lot of well-meaning (yet peripheral), discrete activity and anecdote, rarely turned into actions that made a difference. We wanted data. Hardcore ammunition. We adopted a business-like approach to this phenomenon.

Our unique research was sponsored by 10 'best-in-class' organisations, across sectors as diverse as advertising, law and banking. We reached 2,000 individual women and crunched responses to over 40,000 questions. We ran lively, candid workshops with women who had left and women who had stayed. We listened to their views, and we read reams of insightful, honest, heartfelt and useful feedback outlining their experiences, opinions and learning. Countless awe-inspiring, capable women.

Key things we found:

They're not happy. Assumptions abound about these women. Ladies languishing in blissful splendor, tuning in to BBC Radio 4, volunteering when it suits, nipping to Pilates, meeting for coffee. All quietly content with their lot.

Barmy, outdated, sexist nonsense. Passionate voices yelled the opposite. Their frustration leapt off the page. Women wrote line after line describing wasted skills, thwarted attempts to return, disappointment and disillusionment.

85% of women told us they did want to return. And exactly what is getting in the way.

2. We've had 60 years' experience working with and in businesses that STILL haven't got this sorted.

A bit about us

Lisa Unwin was a partner in Consulting at Arthur Andersen, where she advised clients on large scale change projects. She later became Director of Brand and Communication at Deloitte.

In 2008, she took a career break and helped with numeracy and literacy at a local school, trained as a writer, became a magistrate and spent a lot of time at the school gates. In 2014, keen to return to professional life, she found that opportunities were limited and that she was surrounded by many women who, like her, had taken a break and could simply not return to operate at a level that fulfilled their potential.

Deb Khan has over 18 years' experience running her own business, developing long term relationships with a number of international creative, media and tech companies as well as helping luxury brand clients, architectural practices, leading charities and government departments.

Deb's specialty is people – leadership, creativity, team performance and culture. She has delivered bespoke leadership programmes, helped teams win pitches, led cultural change initiatives and helped redefine the positioning of organisations. She has a background in the creative industries including working at the National Theatre and The Royal Opera House. She has worked as a senior teacher. She has had a lot of jobs and knows a fair bit about non-linear career paths. She has worked with many women in the creative sector, just not enough of them at the top.

Together, Lisa and Deb* bring deep creative and professional expertise. They have seen the same problems and issues play out in organisations as diverse as law firms and advertising agencies. They have a shared passion to do something about it. They set up She's Back and quickly realised they had hit a nerve.

People identified with this frustration. It was their story too. They began to join in the debate, saying:

> **"**This is me" or "my wife", or "my sister", or "my friend "and "This is wrong.**"**

*As we have written this book together, when we describe events in our own lives we refer to ourselves by our first names, Lisa or Deb.

THE STRUCTURE OF THE BOOK

The **first section** of this book is about what's really going on today.

In a **"Manifesto for women"** we talk about why it's important to recognise that women's careers often follow different trajectories from those of men. Lives are long and complex and career opportunities and pathways need to reflect that.

"What's Going on Today" is an antidote to every website we've ever read that makes grand claims for commitments to equality and diversity, whilst in the 'real world' boards are still 80% male. It outlines the difference between corporate rhetoric and reality. It addresses the reasons why progress has been slow and why there is hope that change is possible.

If you find yourself at home wondering what happened to your career, be assured, you're not alone. This chapter explains why we're all in it together.

Section one includes a summary of our research and ends with a chapter called **"Why Work Needs Women"**. A deliberate departure from those well-trodden lines about companies with more women on board performing better. Why? Because that means nothing to the person making a hiring decision; and it means nothing to a woman who is wondering why it seems too difficult to secure the chance to return to a role she can do standing on her head. You need to know the real arguments to make. Why addressing this issue really is important; for you, for work and for the economy.

Section two is more practical. In it we examine the strategies, tools, techniques and tactics that you're going to need to get yourself back. And stay there. It's full of examples, personal stories, lists, exercises all designed to give you some practicable, actionable ideas and motivation.

The stories described are not 'Superwomen'. They are real women who are making mistakes, struggling, having small successes, ploughing on. Women who are inspiring because they want to make a difference and are prepared to help. Women of all ages. Ordinary yet remarkable women.

Finally, we've called the last section **"If Not Now, Then When"**. It's there because, despite the glacial pace of progress over the last twenty years, we really do believe that the time is right for change. The wave of movements around women's rights at work, along with the digital revolution and other macro trends, offer hope that work can and should be done in a different way. One that works better for both women **and** men.

WHO IT'S FOR

We originally wrote this book for women who had taken a career break. Over time, though, we have come to realise that the messages it contains are relevant for a far wider audience. For women who have not taken a break but who might have stepped back or stepped to the side; for men who want to achieve a better work life balance; for anyone who is thinking of taking a break and needs to understand the potential impact on their long-term career.

Where we use the word women, think 'people'.

HOW TO USE IT

We're all busy. The book is designed so that you can read each chapter stand alone. Each chapter will have some prose, outlining our observations about what's going on today and suggesting some actions. The practical chapters all finish with a summary of the action steps we recommend.

We have drawn on the work of many other experts and these are referenced in each chapter. We also suggest where to go for more information and stimulation, and there's a bibliography of other useful resources at the end of the book.

Dip in and out. Complete the exercises when you have the right amount of time. Some of them need you to be able to step away from the chaos that is day to day life; to find the right place and time to create a space for reflection. Time to take stock of the world around you and your place within it.

We are not writing this book because we have navigated our careers perfectly or because we are shining examples of how to build a career that lasts. Far from it. Throughout the book we share stories of people who bring to life the points we are making; they are all real people and they too would be at pains to tell you they made plenty of mistakes. All the stories are real, though some are anonymised due to personal or commercially sensitive reasons.

From time to time, we will introduce articles or thought

pieces that illustrate points in a slightly different way. Here's one about perfection and how much we feel it is over-rated.

WHY FLAWED FEMALES ARE ABSOLUTELY FABULOUS

Inspired by 9 Things Successful Women Never Do

Reading this blog by a female ex-FBI agent (the only woman on her squad) inspired us to put pen to paper. We read the list of the things successful women never do and fell about laughing. We were pretty guilty of all of them. As are many women we know. And yet, we're OK. In fact, we're more than OK. So, let's celebrate our flaws:

1. **Successful women never ignore their fears.** Our tribe, by contrast, are full of them. We're terrified of being found out. Of not being the perfect career woman / parent/partner/worker/housemaker/daughter. We muddle along. We make it up as we go along. It makes us human, approachable & generally nice to be around.

2. **Successful women never run from conflict.** What? Our lives are defined by conflicting demands. We're constantly trying to avoid them blowing up in our face. Don't have time for the hassle. Too much to do.

3. **Successful women never listen to their inner critic.** Forget that. It's one of the loudest voices in our heads. "You're rubbish at craft, don't even bother to try to make the school book day outfit". "That job's out of your reach, you

can only do 90% of what they're looking for". At worst this particular flaw stops us achieving our potential – but it is also what makes us look for help. What drives us to work with others. To help them. To be part of a team.

4. **Successful women never look at their past as a mistake.** Most women we know happily acknowledge lives littered with mistakes. The wrong boyfriend, the wrong choice of degree, the time we didn't put ourselves forward for promotion, when we didn't stand up to a bullying boss, when we didn't stand up against open misogyny at work. You know what? We have a sense of humour. We can laugh at ourselves. Recognising those mistakes makes us more determined to be better in the future – and to stop our daughters making the same mistakes all over again.

5. **Successful women never miss opportunities to shine.** See 4. One of our biggest mistakes, we now realise, is letting others shine; doing all the ground work only for someone else to take the credit and expecting to be recognised simply because of the fabulous work we do. Big mistake.

6. **Successful women never fail to keep their cool.** Ever tried to get a screaming toddler into a pushchair when they are determined to stay out of it? Kept calm when your teenage daughter yells obscenities & slams a door in your face? Smiled at a single work colleague who says, "Leaving early then?" when you walk out of the door at 5 to begin another day's work at home? We are flawed. We lose our tempers. We have a strop, stamp our feet, tear our hair

out. Then we find another flawed woman to whom we can relay our story, have a laugh & move on.

7. **Successful women never fail to do their research.** Nope. What we tend to do is find another fabulously flawed woman, ask her what she'd do/buy/say and then copy that.

8. **Successful women never say quit.**

9. **See what we did there?**

We've made mistakes. We compromise. We put others first. We're human & humble. We put ourselves down far too often. Yes, we need to be far better at shouting out about how fabulous we are. We're utterly, utterly flawed. But boy are we fabulous with it.

The **She's Back** manifesto for women

Manifesto: *(noun)* a written statement of the aims, beliefs and policies of an organization

Our aim is to help women to build meaningful and sustainable careers throughout their working lives.

It's increasingly unlikely that any of us will have careers that begin at 21 and continue steadily until we retire. Whatever your initial ambitions, it's highly likely that there will several bumps and changes of tack along the way. You may end up hating your chosen career, burn out, find a new passion, have health problems, take time out to bring up children, or find yourself looking after elderly relatives. Your career may well need to ebb and flow.

We want to see women build careers which are flexible enough to accommodate their ambitions beyond work, be that around parenting, caring, or other personal goals. Careers which can develop at different speeds, which can deal with breaks and gaps without being permanently thrown off course.

This aim is underpinned by core beliefs:

- Lives are long, complex and messy
- Work adds something to our lives
- Your value is not derived solely through work
- Being a parent develops a new set of skills
- Ageism is pernicious, rife and wrong
- We should be free to make choices

1. Lives are complex and messy

They are also long. Like many women we know, when we graduated we were just as ambitious as the men around us. We were educated. The hard-fought battles around equality were all done and dusted, we had the pill to control our fertility, what could go wrong?

Hitting our thirties. Often, the point at which companies are looking to accelerate the careers of high potential people coincides nicely with the point at which many women are thinking about having children. Yes, many do progress in their careers but sadly others don't.

Lives are long. In *The 100 Year Life*, Lynda Gratton and Andrew Scott explore the many ramifications of us all living for longer. It is increasingly unlikely that any of us – men or women – will have linear careers that encompass one job. We need to be prepared for that.

It should be possible to have careers that twist and turn with our lives, to slow down or accelerate, to step off and then step back, to find fulfilling work throughout our lives.

2. Work adds something to our lives

Work gives you a distinct identity. You're no longer defined as someone's mother, partner or daughter. It can provide structure, meaning, friendship and a sense of community. Learning, being stretched and exercising your brain, are enriching and a very good thing.

Our research proved the major reason for women wanting to return was to find challenging, fulfilling work. Financial reward was a secondary consideration but a very important one. Who amongst us has really saved enough to glide into a comfortable retirement without many years of work ahead?

Women should have the opportunity to find work that makes a difference, is rewarded properly and meets their aspirations and ambitions. We've earned our right to be in the workplace. We deserve to be there. We're valuable and we deserve to be rewarded for the contribution we make.

3. Your value is not solely developed through work

> "When women are strong, families are strong." Hillary Clinton

Work pays far too little attention to the skills and experience people gain outside of the workplace. We look around at the women we know, the women we met through our research, and we marvel at what they've achieved.

They have navigated any number of minefields: brought

up children; cared for elderly or sick relatives; supported partners; held down a job; moved house; moved countries, emerged from a messy divorce; survived serious illness; managed a household; completed years of admin; been a good friend; contributed to the community; and spent years listening to other people and their problems.

None of that is possible without grit, determination, resilience and the ability to innovate, plan, ask for support and learn new skills. They have grown as a result.

4. Being a parent develops important leadership skills

> "Based on my own experience, women will tend to be more inclusive, to reach out more, to care a little more."
> Christine Lagarde, Managing Director, IMF

The world is ever changing. The digital revolution is bringing with it more transparency in business and a need for greater collaboration. Internally and externally. Being open, listening, working with others, helping people, being agile, responsive and flexible – these are traditionally seen as female traits. They're proving invaluable in today's working environment.

As the wonderful **Dr Wanda Austin**, CEO of The Aerospace Corporation, put it on *Woman's Hour* not too long ago, being a mother is all about leadership. You decide the rules, decide what the family has to eat, what manners are expected, how everyone needs to behave.

Mothers have to flex and adapt to the changing needs of their families. They help their children become better people, equipped to thrive as independent, thoughtful adults. This, in a nutshell, is leadership

5. Ageism is pernicious, rife and wrong

We were enraged some time ago, when the newly appointed boss of a well-known high street retailer announced:

> **"I know my customer, she's Mrs M&S, a woman in her 50s who ..."**

Once we calmed down, we questioned his statement, concluding that he had a reductive and myopic view of women like us. We drafted this 'at a glance', hopefully helpful, guide about what she is and isn't, what she likes and dislikes. Ignore at your peril.

Think you know me?

APEROL SPRITZ	NOT	PORT AND LEMON
DAVID BOWIE	NOT	BARRY MANILOW
STIEG LARSSON	NOT	AGATHA CHRISTIE
CARTILAGE RINGS	NOT	ETERNITY RINGS
RED AND GRAZIA	NOT	WOMAN'S WEEKLY
CAITLIN MORAN	NOT	CLAIRE RAYNER
SPIN CLASSES	NOT	KEEP FIT
CATHERINE CAWOOD	NOT	JULIET BRAVO
OMBRE AND BALAYAGE	NOT	BLUE RINSE AND PERM

6. People should be free to make choices

The last thought for this chapter is that we would love to see women be free to make choices. At times, it doesn't always feel as though there are options and that feels wrong. Equally, there can be pressure to make a particular choice at a particular time. To go back to work. To stay at home and be there to bring up your children. To be the one who takes care of an elderly relative. To sacrifice your career because your partner has to relocate.

Let's be more conscious of the choices we make. And let's try to be supportive of others and hold our judgements for another time.

Why the Long Game

Whatever your situation now or in the future, our advice is always to have an eye on the long term. Beware making short term decisions that limit your long-term options. Treat your career like a game of chess.

PLAY THE LONG GAME

We often read articles outlining the outrageous cost of childcare and the role it plays in mothers' decisions to leave their full-time jobs.

Take care. Making what appear to be financially smart short-term moves can prove damaging in the long run. Instead, imagine that your future – both personal and professional – is one very important game of chess.

1. Think like a chess master

A chess master doesn't resign from the game simply because she is in a tricky situation. She thinks strategically, planning three or four moves ahead. She has an eye on the end game.

Your decision to give up a full-time job might make sense today, not just financially but emotionally too. But will that decision enable you to play the role you want, living a life you love, in the long term?

Having young children is a **temporary condition**. As one working mother put it: "Seeing my daughter start senior school made me really think about what I was going to do with the next twenty years of my working life, something I had given zero thought to when she was 6 and I resigned from a great job."

Your children will not be young forever. Have a long-term plan.

2. Adapt your tactics as the game progresses

Chess, much like your career, is a long game with a beginning, middle and end.

The first phase of chess is busy. There are lots of pieces on the board and you need to get moving to position yourself tactically for the future. It's the same when you start work. Along with your peers, you dig in and work long hours, establish yourself, build your network.

As the game progresses, things change. Children come along who need and deserve attention. It is during this middle phase that a grand chess master stands out from the crowd because of her ability to devise cunning strategies; to take risks and to be creative.

Mothers who need flexibility have to be able to negotiate it without their careers paying a heavy price. Too often, 'part time' becomes synonymous with 'unambitious' and precludes women from taking on more responsibility. Be creative about defining your role and contribution, take risks, be prepared to be measured on output and not hours worked. The benefits to your long-term career will be immense.

Your goal from the beginning? Plan, adapt, position. Stay in the game. Play to win.

3. Be prepared to sacrifice some pieces, but always plan a few moves ahead

As the grand master of your own life it is inevitable that you will need to make sacrifices. Think carefully about what pieces you are willing and able to put aside along the way to manoeuvre yourself into a winning end-game position.

That might mean taking a different role or perhaps going part-time. It could entail a sacrifice – passing up a promotion maybe. If so, make sure you are not written off for promotions and choice assignments over the long term. Seek out a mentor or a sponsor who will look out for you in the future. Position yourself to make your next big move a winning one by maintaining and growing your networks.

Be prepared to lose some battles if you want to win the war.

4. Remember, the queen is not the only piece on the board

Yes, she's important. Powerful. A great multi-tasker. But there may be a king as well. On the same side of the board as you. Wearing the same colours. You need to have a shared view of what 'winning' looks like. And you need to work together.

5. Be a player

Women are creating lives as working mothers that suit them – for now and with an eye toward their future. Certainly, they have to be focused and tenacious. They must take it on themselves to negotiate the role they want. If they cannot work five days a week, they make up for it with their quality and delivery. They have the confidence that comes from knowing their value as professionals, and from continuing to develop that value, even when they are at home.

Many women still see their career as a series of reactive moves, responding to circumstances as best they can. But if you think like a chess master, that begins to change.

There's a bigger game to be played than work-life balance. It's the game of creating your life, one move at a time, designed to set up all the people and organizations – your partner, children, clients, employers, and network – to give you the opportunities, support, and guidance that you need to succeed each step of the way.

How one architect went from the Olympics to the design & build of her own career

Kay is an architect whose career highlights include being Head of Design for the London 2012 Olympics. The twists and turns of her working life perfectly illustrate the ups and downs of a long and ultimately successful career.

Her early career included working on the Barcelona Olympics and a stint at a large architectural practice. When her children were small she took a high profile role at the Foreign and Commonwealth Office. The downside was a gruelling travel schedule and very low residual salary. Why did she do it?

"My husband's career was taking off. My role as a mother was feeding and bedtimes. It didn't feel enough. I wanted a dynamic, exciting challenge and the new job was just what I was looking for, I loved it."

It proved a smart strategic move. In 2006 Kay became Head of Design for the London 2012 Olympics delivery team. The scale and tight time pressure of designing the (brilliant) Olympic Park from scratch cannot be underestimated.

On a personal level, though, Kay was exhausted, mentally and physically. She had severe carpal tunnel syndrome in both wrists making work impossible. She decided to take a break.

"Work was impossible and my home life was in chaos. And

I wanted to spend more time with my children as they approached their teens. I took a break, but it was a shock. I'd suddenly gone from being a decision maker to loading the dishwasher regularly. I felt a strange sense of loss."

Kay made sure that even when she wasn't in permanent employment, she kept active in a way that meant she would, in time, be able to return.

"I maintained my network and was asked by old colleagues to help on some projects including one for Crossrail. I participated in design reviews and competitions. It meant people saw me regularly. I never totally disappeared."

At the age of 55 Kay is ready to step up again. She is studying for an MSc in Infrastructure Investment and Finance, and she's part of an all-female collective who have recently won a highly prestigious countryside development competition.

Her advice for anyone thinking of returning after a break?

"Being at home can really erode your confidence. But don't be put off. As soon as you engage again you discover that you still have all the skills and abilities you once had."

Kay and the Long Game

Chess moves	Kay's positioning/moves	Lessons learned
First moves	<ul><li>Complete professional training</li><li>Secure work for prestigious client</li><li>Start family</li><li>Keep working</li></ul>	All the juggling was tough, but I was young and had the energy and drive
Middle game 1	<ul><li>Secure career enhancing role at Foreign & Commonwealth</li><li>Sacrifices ("pieces given up") – time with children who were toddlers.</li><li>Salary not as lucrative as elsewhere</li><li>Led on to Head of Design at Olympics</li></ul>	My partner's career was taking off and had priority. But I was still personally ambitions, so I was happy to make those sacrifices. I loved the job and it ultimately helped me get the Olympic gig.
The end game?	<ul><li>Burnt out, physically and mentally</li><li>Teenage children needed her</li><li>Chaos at home</li><li>Time to leave work</li></ul>	Sometimes you just need to be there. I wanted to bond with my kids before they left home.
Middle game 2	<ul><li>Use contacts to build up project work</li><li>Maidenhead town council & other new clients for freelance work</li><li>Became judge for design competitions</li><li>Started MSC</li></ul>	I needed to rest and get better. I also needed to keep relevant and connected. Using contacts to slowly build up a stream of freelance work meant I never really disappeared.
The next phase	<ul><li>Landing successful roles chairing a number of large scale building projects</li><li>Involved in VeloCity – consortium which has recently won countryside development competition.</li></ul>	

Applying the long game to your career so far

The second section of this book is all about tactics, plans and actions. Before you launch into those, we recommend taking time to reflect on your career journey so far. This template is designed to help.

Stage of Game	Example questions to consider	Your thoughts
Early moves	● What was your plan? ● Skills acquired? ● Early positioning	
Strength of your position	● Professional qualifications? ● Technical expertise? ● Reputation? ● Relationships? ● Performance? ● Networks? ● Knowledge?	
Challenges	● Doubts about future direction? ● Conflicting ambitions (e.g. family & work) ● Time at work v time for self: out of balance?	
Middle game	● What tactics did you deploy? ● Were they driven by short term considerations? ● How did your long term aims influence you? ● Did you have to make any sacrifices? ● How did that feel? ● Was it worth it? ● Did you have tactics to compensate for the sacrifices? ● How did the rest of your team help (or not)?	

Stage of Game	Example questions to consider	Your thoughts
The End Game	• Where do you feel you are today? Still in the middle? • Do you have a view of what the end game might look like? • Do you have a plan to get there? • What resources do you need? • What tactics? • What plans? • How are the rest of your team going to help	

Should I stay, or should I go? Why this social and public sector professional decided to play the long game.

Sutiyah has always been passionate about social justice and began her career in the charitable sector. She had her first child relatively young and not long after, pregnant with her second, moved to a private sector consultancy. She felt pressure to take a career break at that point but rejected the idea.

"It was an important career pivot point for me, and my husband was in the middle of his professional qualifications. We could at least share the child care. It felt right to keep going."

The infrastructure and climate around working mums was not as supportive as it is today. Working 4 days a week she was the only parent below partner and also the youngest in the team. Despite this, the trade-offs were worth it.

"I had a really supportive husband. I was able to work on

assignments that included international travel. It was all doable."

Sutiyahi began to question her long term ambitions. Whilst the private sector was interesting and lucrative, she felt it was time to return to her real passion and left to return to the social sector.

"If you're going to be away from your kids 4 days a week, the work has got to be worth it."

However, things changed as her two boys were approaching senior school and the weekends felt 'too stretched' for all the things that came with this.

"This time it felt different. The boys were moving schools and from a career perspective if felt as though I could afford to take time out. I'd established my reputation enough that I could take a break and prioritise my family. In a way, I'd reaped the benefits of going back so early in my career after the boys were born."

She found people's reactions interesting.

"Whilst some people were positive, others kept asking why, as though I was making a huge mistake. It took me some time stop reacting, to be pressured into explaining myself and accept that it was actually more than okay to invest time in my family and myself."

A year later, Sutiyah is now starting to phase back into work. She is open to what the future might hold and feels stronger for the time out.

Her conclusion:

"I think we need to normalise the idea that women have different options at different times in their lives. Whether you stay at home for the early years or play the long game, or a bit of both – it shouldn't be so binary."

3.

What's going on today

At pretty much every organisation we've seen, the proportion of women at different levels of seniority looks something like this:

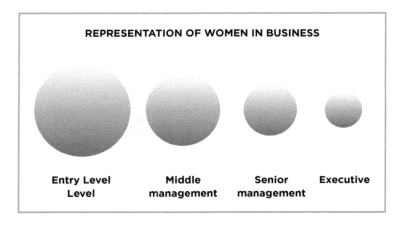

REPRESENTATION OF WOMEN IN BUSINESS

| Entry Level Level | Middle management | Senior management | Executive |

This pattern is verified by various studies and reviews. The 2017 Hampton Alexander review found that women held less than a fifth of Executive Committee positions in the FTSE 100 and only 16.6% of such roles in the FTSE 250. A 2017 McKinsey/Lean In review found a similar pattern in America.

Something is going on to hamper women's progression through the ranks. One factor, we hear from many women, is motherhood.

WHY MOTHERHOOD HOLDS US BACK

Don't get us wrong. We do love to hear success stories. Women who've made it. Men who embrace flexible working. Companies succeeding in their efforts to change their gender balance. However, sometimes the success stories are so loud they drown out the experience of the thousands of real women who **are** struggling. The final straw was an article headed *Multinational Director reveals why motherhood NEVER held her back*. Here's our (all too real) alternative version:

Woman next door reveals why motherhood RUINED her career.

1. She got pregnant and couldn't travel so was taken off a high-profile assignment – even though the technology was there to enable remote working

2. On maternity leave, her clients were handed over to others (who never gave them back)

3. Her peers were offered places on a fast-track leadership programme. She was offered a maternity coach

4. Her request to go to 4 days a week was accepted (eventually) but her workload didn't actually change

5. Still, she was so grateful to be able to have that one

day at home that she fitted the work in at evenings and weekends. But was only paid for the 4 days of course.

6. Her pay rises decreased in size every year.

7. Promotion opportunities were non-existent (she was 'part-time'). Peers moved up; her career flatlined.

8. She missed all the networking opportunities – drinks in the evenings & cycling at the weekends not being great if you have toddlers to look after, a partner who's not sharing the burden and parents who live 200 miles away.

9. She was always late for that critical 8am team meeting on a Thursday morning.

10. She quit/was fired/put up with it ... you choose.

Whilst we applaud and celebrate those who make it work, and organisations who are trying very hard to change things, let's not ignore what is still the reality for thousands of women with children and careers.

We're starting with that article because it represents the truth of many women's experience. It's by no means a universal experience but sadly it is all too common. What are the impacts on women's careers?

- Women's careers being cut short
- A lack of women at the top, across all sectors
- A persistent gender pay gap
- Women doing jobs they are way over-qualified for, jobs they could frequently do with their eyes closed

- Women taking career breaks that end up lasting forever

- Limited options when women want to return

Fortunately, all of this is well recognised. The impact on women's careers, and problems caused by lack of representation of women, are not going unnoticed. Far from it. Enlightened, well intentioned people are doing lots to help.

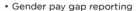

- Gender pay gap reporting
- Right to request flexible working
- Shared parental leave
- Women's Business Council

- Quotas
- Targets
- Diversity & inclusion dept
- Unconscioius bias training
- Transparency of reporting

- Women's networks
- Self-help books
- Coaches
- Female role models

- Women in leadership programme
- Mentors
- Sponsors
- Assertiveness training
- Returnships

The Government has stepped in, forcing companies to report on the gender pay gap, and there isn't a day goes by without the press making a comment about women in business.

The pure waste of talent is also not going unnoticed. We will elaborate in later chapters on the people and programmes who are taking action to help more women find work.

Yet, despite ambitious targets, verbal commitment from

senior leaders, millions being spent on 'diversity and inclusion' initiatives and plenty of media attention being focused on the subject of women in business, the status quo more or less prevails. Progress is slow. It can still feel like a battle for the majority of women trying to navigate careers and family.

> **"**If you know the enemy and know yourself, you need not fear the result of 100 battles. If you know yourself but not the enemy, for every victory gained, you will also suffer a defeat.**"**
> Lao Tsu, The Art of War

We see 5 factors which are hindering progress.

1. Rhetoric versus reality

There is a lot of talk in organisations about 'commitment to diversity'. But is this talk backed up by behaviour and actions on the ground?

Another way of putting this is to talk about 'espoused theory' versus 'theory in use'. These concepts were explored in the work of Argyris and Schon on organisational behaviour.

What do we mean by this? **Espoused values** put simply, are the values people **believe** their behaviour is based on.

Values-in-use on the other hand, are the values implied by their behaviour and actions.

In short, leaders may believe they value diversity, for example (and this is backed up by written commitments) but somewhere down the line actual behaviours and decisions demonstrate the opposite.

As one client recently put it:

> **"**The values on our website are great. It's the street values that are not.**"**

2. Lack of Flexibility

There are very few organisations that don't have flexible working policies. Anyone who has been working for an employer for 26 weeks or more has the legal right, in the UK, to request flexible working. So how come it's still relatively rare? How is it that so many women tell us their requests to work flexibly have been turned down?

And where flexible working has been granted, why is it that it seems to come with consequences for career progression and promotion. As one woman told us:

> **"**The firm was fantastic at finding flexible working arrangements that suited me. But I went from being a top performer to constantly being graded 'meets expectations'. I really don't think my performance was any different and wasn't prepared to stay where my contribution just wasn't valued.**"**

Research by Claudia Goldin, an economist at Harvard, has studied the gender pay gap and found that one major cause is a 'penalty' for flexible working. She studied men and women working in the same profession and found that the average hourly rate of those working part time (largely women) was significantly less than those working full time. In effect, in accepting flexible working arrangements, women were accepting a disproportionate reduction in their pay.

When you consider that subsequent pay rises are usually a fixed percentage of base pay, this means that, all else being equal, that pay gap will rise as wages rise over time.

3. Diversity deniers

There are plenty of senior, and not so senior, influential people around who genuinely do not perceive a lack of diversity at senior levels to be a problem. Some think the battle is over, others view any attempts to address some of the issues faced by women and minorities as being 'positive discrimination', left leaning and political correctness gone a bit mad.

The chairman of a global ad agency and a tech engineer were both recently forced out of their positions when they made their views public. The first claimed that women were happy not to progress too far, their ambitions lying elsewhere; the other stated that women were biologically unsuited to technical roles.

Both were castigated in the media and their careers suffered as a result. But – hold your breath here – were they only daring to articulate what many others may believe but keep quiet about? There are many more like them who do not speak out in public but do act in line with their views on a day-to-day basis. They may, in public, appear supportive but in private they too think diversity efforts are, at best, a distraction or, at worst, positively damaging to business.

4. We have a Diversity Programme. It's sorted.

It's rare for us to come across an organisation without a Head of Diversity. Or Diversity & Inclusion or some other similar title. Often, these roles frequently sit in HR departments. Is this the right place? If they are so critical, should they not sit with the CEO? Or more radically, should there be a programme at all? Here's a common refrain.

> "Our diversity programme has been going for years. We've tried a bunch of initiatives. Nothing really seems to make a huge difference."

'Programmes' often come with unintended consequences. They feel like they are 'someone else's job', they sit on the side of the organisation, away from business as usual. And if they are labelled 'Diversity' it can be taken to mean 'not relevant for white men' and are thus not taken very seriously.

5. There is an underlying assumption that the 'problem' is the women.

Delve into the detail of diversity programmes and many are designed to 'fix' the women. They coach them and mentor them, teach them to flourish in a man's world. Leadership programmes often encourage them to adopt typically male behavioural traits in order to compete and win. What effort goes into working out which elements of organisational behaviour need to be fixed?

Yes, unconscious bias training is available, but what about going beyond that? We struggle to find examples of companies actively championing the needs of women working part-time with clients, supporting and promoting them as still valuable assets. A tough question from one ex consultant:

> "Where's the part when consulting firms tell clients 'We value diversity so much that we want you to know that some of our partners and senior people work part-time. They will let you know their working arrangements and we ask that you respect their non-working days. We know they will deliver for you'."

Harsh but fair?

6. Women 'giving up' and doing it for themselves

Finally, we see women looking at organisational life, admitting defeat, and looking for a 'third way'. Making a conscious choice to leave the corporate world and find a way of working which enables them to fulfil their other life ambitions.

SISTERS DOING IT FOR THEMSELVES

Pilates instructor   Learning support

Volunteering

Part-time job   **Yoga teacher**

Life coach   **NSPCC**

Retraining

"Mumpreneur"   **PTA**

Magistrate

Creative writing course

Hand-made baby   **Cup cake business**
clothes

Masters   **School administrator**

Blogging   **Looking for work**

Campaign activist   **Business coach**

The variety of activity that women engage in is enormous.
Melanie Eusebe left a 17-year career as a management
consultant so that she could follow her passion – she co-
founded the highly influential and much admired Black British
Business Awards.

> **"**I've always wanted to start my own
> business and do my own thing. I love
> having the flexibility to work when
> and where I want and to manage my
> own time and resources. It's really
> empowering.**"**

Jane was a classic example of Sheryl Sandberg's assertion that women "leave before they leave". She had joined a strategy consulting team as a new graduate: smart, ambitious, driven.

Some years in, she looked upwards and could see no way of combining a career as a consultant with being a mother. Working long hours, having to travel at the drop of a hat, working away from home 40 weeks of the year. Knowing that having a family was important to her, she quit and retrained as an interior designer. Using her diverse set skills acquired in consulting she built her business from scratch and ended up with some lucrative commissions that included high-end London residential and super yachts. When she did eventually become pregnant with twins she managed to mothball the business and pick it up again. She is tenacious enough that her business then survived a move to a new family home in South Yorkshire, where she had to redefine her proposition once again to be able to maintain her client base in London.

Mel and Jane are great examples of women taking their ambition and their skills and finding a different way to deploy them, because traditional work environments cannot accommodate them. This, surely, is a loss to all the potential employers out there. Many women do the same, performing useful and interesting work, which, sadly is not always particularly profitable. And if these women decide they want to return to more lucrative employment, they find the skills and experience they have gained doing these activities are not valued by organisations. Which means many end up working independently or in small businesses, lost to the senior corporate roles that might actually benefit from their expertise.

Going back to the bubble diagram at the top of this chapter, the women haven't disappeared, they are here working on their own.

GETTING YOU BACK

Some women have no desire to return to corporate life. But many do. They find themselves at stage where they look ahead and recognise they have 20-odd years of career potential ahead of them and want to do something with it. We need more women who have stepped out of or stepped back from professional careers to find ways back in. And we need work to recognise that this is a valuable talent pool that cannot be ignored.

It is happening. There is hope. Trust us.

We're going to tell you about the things you can do to accelerate your progress back to work and how your experience during your break can make you stronger on your return.

You'll hear stories of people who've done just that. Jenni, who returned to teaching after a 10-year break; Emma, who felt she had one more, big full-time role in her after 11 years of working on interim projects; and David, who reframed his attitude to work and identity following a break to care for his disabled son.

We'll tell you about VeloCity, a group of women in building who formed their own network and won one of the most prestigious design competitions in the UK.

And more importantly we'll tell YOU what you can do to plot your own return. You ARE in demand, work does want more women. They just don't always know how to find them. Roll your sleeves up and be prepared. We're not saying it's easy, but it definitely is possible. Get stuck in.

WHY WOMEN ARE IN DEMAND

Here's something interesting. We've recently been approached by some small(ish) businesses who have a problem: finding the talent they need to help them grow.

"We need someone to refocus our brand & get our message out to the market."

"We need help professionalising our business operations."

"We have to beef up our business development activities."

Pleas from a B2B services organisation, a tech start-up which is now growing, and a digital media business. What we love is that they all talk about the work that needs doing, rather than a job with a long list of tasks and activities.

Another thing they had in common was that they all thought a woman returning after a break could be the ideal solution. Why?

- **You're brilliantly organised** and will use your time

effectively. You have fantastic time management skills. You know how to work a deadline. These business leaders are looking for someone who will focus on results and get the job done.

- **You're resourceful.** They are growing quickly. Their leaders don't have time to plan this work to the nth level of detail – hence there is no long task list. You have 20 years plus of varied experience – in work and out of it. You will be creative and think laterally about how to get things done. Perfect.

- **You're hungry.** After years of putting other people first (and putting yourself down) it's your time. You want your career back and boy will you work hard.

- **You're a cost-effective hire.** Why hire someone full-time as a default when the work that needs doing can be done in less time by someone experienced and efficient. This doesn't mean you're cheap or have no alternatives. It means you focus on what needs to be done and get it done as efficiently as possible.

- **You're an investment not a liability.** You've had plenty of training throughout your career; you're self-aware; you work well in a team; you're mature; you can safely be left to handle the problematic CEO of a client; you don't need a tremendous amount of supervision.

- **Your difference is your strength.** Ideas are better, the environment is more fun when there's a bit of variety. And when women come along as potential candidates in the future, the business will look so much more attractive for having you there. As Marcus Wildsmith, co-founder of Cutover, a fintech scale up business, put it:

"We were up to 14 people, but we were all men. As a leadership team we agreed that we really needed to hire a great woman. Otherwise, somewhere down the line the best candidate for a job would be a woman and they wouldn't even interview with us."

So, come on ladies, work needs you.

4

She's Back
research

We set up She's Back with a hypothesis: that there were thousands of experienced, talented women who had stepped away from successful careers and who would return if only they could.

The purpose of our research was to test that hypothesis.

This chapter sets out:

- What the research set out to do
- The methodology used
- A profile of the women who contributed
- What they said
- Results of our follow up research
- Why this matters

RESEARCH OBJECTIVES

The objectives were quite straightforward. Women have been graduating from university in roughly equal numbers to men since the 1960s and yet seem to disappear when you look at the senior levels in organisations. The questions were:

- Why do they leave?
- Would they consider returning?
- If so, why?
- What is getting in the way?
- What would they need to make a successful return?

RESEARCH METHODOLOGY

The first step was to gather support, which turned out to be relatively straightforward. Businesses were just as interested as we were in the answers to these questions, as was Dr Thomas Calvard of the University of Edinburgh Business School, who agreed to support the project.

Research took place between February and April 2015 and covered women from a variety of sectors, including print media, advertising, insurance, law, banking, consulting and the public sector. The project was sponsored by five blue chip organisations including Allen & Overy, AXA and News UK.

The aim was to gather the views of women who had reached a relatively senior level before leaving to take a career break, through face to face workshops and interviews and a bespoke online survey.

Workshops were simple to organise, convivial and well-attended. The online survey was a different beast. With such a large employee base Lisa and Deb had assumed that organisations would find it simple to contact their female alumni and ask for their views. Not so. Leave aside the complications of data protection and the legalities of contacting people without their express permission, and the biggest problem was the relationship the women often had with their old employer. There was none.

Even when an organisation had a formal alumni network, many of the women who had left to take career breaks were not active in that network and were therefore tremendously difficult to reach.

Not to be deterred, we hustled and cajoled, built a network of support online, found opportunities to get a bit of PR to spread the word and learnt how to use Twitter and Hootsuite, identifying who else could help.

Eventually, the online survey, which ran for 8 weeks, reached over 1,300 women. It contained 18 questions along with plenty of space for open comment.

A PROFILE OF THE WOMEN

The average age of the women was 41, with most being spread like this:

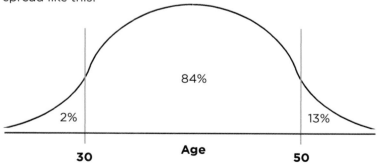

84%

2%

13%

Age

30   **50**

On average, they had 12 years' experience before taking a break: some less, many a fair bit more. Think about that. After 12 years of experience most people would not only have developed plenty of technical and managerial capability, they would have also built up a substantial amount of social capital: client relationships, industry networks and the like.

Women were also asked about their level of seniority prior to taking a break.

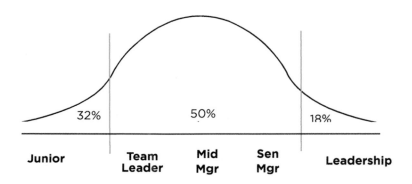

68% were at team leader level or above before taking a break, 57% were middle manager and above. As predicted, most left before reaching the levels at which they could be considered potential candidates for Executive Board level.

WHAT THE WOMEN TOLD US

1. Why they left

85% of the women who contributed told us they had taken a break for family related reasons. These included an inability to juggle work and family, the cost of childcare and employers being unreceptive to requests for flexibility and part-time working.

Some women actually left their jobs even before they had a family, best summed up in these quotes from two lawyers:

"I was working such long hours that if I didn't leave, there was no way I was going to get a boyfriend let alone start a family."

"I didn't see anyone above me, man or woman, balancing work and family in a way that I could aspire to. So I left."

There are other reasons, clearly. Some women had been made redundant; others had relocated to move with their partner to a different region or country; some had to leave because of their own ill health or to take care of a sick relative. However, the biggest problem was the conflict between having a career and being a parent.

2. Their attitudes to returning

85% of women said they wanted to return to work, either immediately or at some point in the future. By far the largest proportion – 55% – said they wanted to return now.

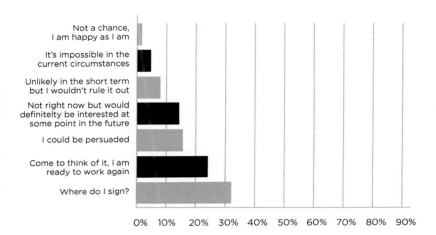

Their motivation? First and foremost, personal fulfilment. Money was important, but it was secondary for most women after finding challenging work which would enable them to make an impact.

92% said they wanted to be fully engaged with the organisation they returned to, and 65% wanted to be back on a career track. They were not done with their careers.

3. The biggest barrier to returning?

A lack of flexibility in the workplace.

The need for flexibility was paramount in almost every response. It means different things to different people – part-time work, the ability to work from home part of the time, term time contracts, the possibility of stepping off a career ladder and then back on again. But there was a clear perception that most workplaces are inflexible and are stuck in a culture of presenteeism.

4. What do women need in order to return?

91% asked for trust.

"Trust in me to get the job done and to arrange my work around my family."

These are 35 to 45-year-old women, with years of experience behind them, many of whom have been in management positions in the past. Most are parents. Is this such an impossible ask?

Faced with a choice of other factors that could support their return – being part of a cohort of similar people, access to a coach, having a mentor, being provided with technical training etc – women were clear about the number 1 factor that would make their return a success:

88% chose "A manager who wants me to succeed" as their number one.

5. How they felt

This was a long survey, with 18 questions in total. Yet almost 20% of women who completed it also went on to add additional comments. A common theme was a sense of frustration at just how difficult it is proving to return to challenging, decently paid work.

"I believe this is a catastrophic waste of skills."

SUBSEQUENT RESEARCH

We subsequently conducted two further pieces of research.

1. Women in Management Consulting

The first was with the Management Consultancies Association and 4 large consulting firms, including IBM and PwC. This time we were looking specifically at women who'd worked in Consulting – why they left and where they went – in order to inform their own efforts around gender diversity.

This research reached over 600 women. The results followed a similar pattern, except that the need to travel at a moment's notice was an extra factor making women choose to leave the sector. Other key findings were:

- 77% of women had spent more than 5 years in consulting before they left, with 19% having 12 or more years of experience.
- 70% were manager grade or above when they left.
- Even if they took a break, most subsequently found employment, but most (86%) did not return to work for a large consulting firm, instead finding roles back in industry, with small consultancies or within the private sector.

The lack of flexibility was again a key factor in women choosing to leave the sector but here the tone of the story was somewhat different, perhaps best summed up by this quote:

"My current employer welcomes skilled, educated and motivated individuals

> from consultancy and was prepared to pay comparable packages with flexible and sustainable working patterns. **"**

During the workshops we ran with women who'd left, what became clear was that these were highly capable women who were choosing to take the skills they'd acquired and use them elsewhere. Not surprising when you consider the demographic of respondents, most of whom were manager grade or above. At that level you've acquired a decent mix of skills. Along with technical competence you're likely to be able to have a broad set of other competencies, including:

- Risk management
- Project management
- Team leadership
- Planning and reporting
- Sales
- Client relationship development

Little wonder their skills were in demand.

2. How Women Return

The second, smaller piece of research was self-initiated. We were curious about how women did manage to return after a break, so we reached out to our growing network and asked them.

We heard from over 250 women across a variety of sectors. The key message? Word of mouth and contacts work much better than recruitment agencies as a route back to work. Whilst 50% had tried recruiters, only 9% found their job that way. 44% found a job through word of mouth or through a personal referral.

Most reported that they have more flexibility in their new role, but also report less responsibility and fewer opportunities for training and career development. It would appear that it isn't just pay that has to be sacrificed when women choose to put a need for flexibility at the forefront of their career choices.

WHY THIS MATTERS

Talented, experienced women are struggling to return to work if they take a career break. When they do return, they are often working below the level of their full potential as they need flexibility and their careers pay a price. This matters.

It matters for women because they want to work for organisations who know they need access to the best talent, and it matters to our economy. Economic growth has been low and productivity levels have stagnated in the UK over the last 10 years. Having talented, experienced people sitting on the sidelines, unable to return to work – or indeed working below their potential and unable to progress – makes no sense. On any level.

5.

Why work needs women

> **❝**We're making great strides on our diversity targets everywhere. Except around senior women. Progress is too slow. And when we try to recruit we just can't find them.**❞**
>
> Head of Consulting, Global Professional Services

In this chapter we will:

1. Confirm the business case for having more women at all levels
2. Pinpoint the crux of the problem: why, despite an apparently clear business case, are there still too few women around?
3. Suggest how women can use this business case to their advantage

THE BUSINESS CASE FOR HAVING MORE WOMEN AT ALL LEVELS

There is a bottom-line benefit to having a more diverse workforce. The 2018 McKinsey report *Diversity Matters* found that gender diverse companies were 15% more likely to outperform their competition, whilst ethnically and racially diverse companies were 35% more likely to outperform.

Diversity is about much more than gender. The focus of *this* book is predominantly on women as that has been the basis of our research and our experience.

Credit Suisse produced one of the most frequently cited and pivotal pieces of research on the topic. You may well have seen this quote on more than one occasion:

> **"**Findings from Credit Suisse show that the average return on equity of companies with at least one woman on the board between 2006 and 2012 was 16% compared with 12% for firms without female board representation.**"**

These are just two examples of research reports: there are several more where they came from. Which explains why Government bodies, individual organisations, industry bodies and regulators are beginning to set targets for women in different areas:

● From 6th April 2017 employers in Great Britain with more than 250 staff are required by law to publish the annual figures on their own website and on a Government website. This information will cover the gender pay gap and include bonus gap (mean and median averages), show the proportion of men and women receiving bonuses and the proportion of men and women in their pay structure. Although we anticipate a bumpy few years, this transparency will be the basis of a positive shift.

- As of July 2017, 141 UK Financial Institutions had signed up to the Government's *Women in Finance Charter* which includes setting targets for women at senior levels and reporting on those targets.

- The Hampton Alexander review has set a target for FTSE 100 companies to have 33% of women on FTSE 350 Boards by 2020.

- Accenture has pledged to "grow the percentage of women we hire to at least 40% worldwide by 2017."

- GE recently announced a gender diversity target: it announced a goal to hire 20,000 women in STEM roles by the year 2020.

- The IPA have asked members to sign up to *Make the Leap* which includes a pledge to aim for 40% representation of women in senior positions by 2020.

Antonio Lucio, Chief Marketing Officer of Hewlett Packard recently explained his commitment to diversity:

> "Our bet is that when the staff we have adequately represent the populations we serve our output will improve. It delivers a higher innovation rate. We believe that having a more diverse team in place will translate into better work, no question."

Hewlett Packard now refuse to work with agencies who cannot deliver a diverse team onto their account.

The reason Lucio and others like him are so committed to having diverse teams is that they understand exactly why having more women delivers such benefits to business. They understand these common sense reasons:

- **Representing the customer base.** Over 75% of consumer decisions are made by women. Mimicking the customer and client base allows you to design products and services that appeal to your customers and sell faster

- **The brain drain costs.** Companies spend a fortune hiring and training brilliant female graduates only to see them walk out of the door 7 or 8 years down the line.

- **Being held to account**. Increased transparency through social media means people can take a proper look at companies, what they do and who works there. A lack of senior women can make younger women think twice.

- **The loss of invaluable social and intellectual capital.** Women take with them many years of deep trusted relationships and experience when they leave

- **A lack of diversity of thought.** The people remaining with have a tendency to think and act the same – there is a danger of groupthink.

- **A danger of looking neolithic**. All men at the top? Even the most traditional of organisations – the Conservative party, the IMF, the Bank of England – don't look like that. It's old fashioned, odd and not reflective of modern working environments or society.

- **Pitches are lost** if you present with an all-male te
team needs to reflect your clients and their custo
Selection panels are rarely single sex and look unfavorably
on sales teams who are.

- **You're fishing in a limited pool.** Evidence proves there is
a huge pool of untapped talent out there. Brilliant women
who would work hard, not faff about all day, get stuff done
and be deeply loyal.

- **The future is all about flexibility and collaboration.**
Technology has only just begun to affect how we
work. Succeeding in a connected world requires agility,
communication, flexibility and collaboration. Things that
most women like and traditionally demonstrate as strengths.

- **Your responsibility.** Doing the right thing, standing up
to your corporate responsibilities, is frequently being
referenced as a business differentiator.

HOW TO USE THE BUSINESS CASE TO YOUR ADVANTAGE

This is a hot topic and many organisations feel they are not
making enough progress.

"With 80 people queuing up for every vacancy here, why
should I give a job to a returning woman who's maybe
had a 2 or 3-year career break? Or someone who wants
flexibility versus someone who's prepared to work full time? I
understand why we need to have more women, but we have
an immediate pressure of filling the roles."

The key is to position yourself as part of the solution.

Do your research on attitudes, targets, pledges, league tables and awards. Hone your knowledge about commitments that have been made in your sector or by the organisation you are targeting. What are their own clients and suppliers doing? What are their competitors up to?

Think about the following for any organisation you're set to apply to:

1. Have targets been set for the proportion of women in the organisation or sector you're looking to work in? Are these in the public domain, mainstream and social? Could your hire be used to amplify their commitments?

2. Do they proudly present their credentials on their website? Are they applying for awards, winning them and then celebrating them?

3. Comparing the targets they claim and the stats shown in their annual report, how are they doing? What level of diversity do they have today? Has it shifted at all in recent years?

4. Is it possible to compare them with another company in the same sector that has a better/worse reputation in terms of diversity of talent?

5. Is the industry body actively encouraging their members to increase representation of women?

6. Who are the clients? And their customers? How will you – by adding to the diversity of their team – enhance revenues? (An example in marketing is that many

marketing managers who hold budgets are now women and diverse teams appeal more)

7. On a commercial front, could your hire help increase retention of other, more junior, women by providing a role model and mentor above them in the organisation?

8. If you are going to be working on a flexible basis, how does that impact the overall cost base?

It may become apparent when answering these questions that they're not actively seeking or encouraging women at all levels. If that's the case – perhaps focus your energies elsewhere. Life is sometimes too short.

HOW A FINTECH SCALE UP WENT FROM 0% TO 22% WOMEN IN 5 MONTHS

Early in 2017, we were approached by Marcus Wildsmith, cofounder of Cutover, a fintech business that helps firms switch business critical IT systems. He, along with his partner, had nursed the company through two incubator programs, secured second-round funding and had six multinational clients. The team was up to 14 people, all men, most of whom had been attracted by word-of-mouth.

"We're at the stage of growth now," said Wildsmith "where we really need to make sure our core business processes are in order. We have plenty of technical skills on the team, but it feels as though we are ready for a quasi-COO. But we need to be careful we don't burn too much cash too quickly and it doesn't feel like a full-time role right now."

Usually in these cases, leaders see two choices. Option one is recruiting an established COO.

A safe move but an expensive one when you take into account a premium salary to lure an experienced player to a small organisation, and the need to give away equity and hefty recruitment fees.

Then there's option two. Hire someone who hasn't yet reached executive level – maybe an accountant who has seen how things work in large organizations, who is keen to learn and just needs a little supervision. Or a lot. That's the risk. In startups, time comes close to cash as something in short supply.

But Wildsmith recognized there was a third option in the overlooked talent pool of women who have taken a break from professional life and now want to return to the workplace. These are women with all the experience he was looking for, who will work hard to get the job done in the hours it takes.

They have experience delivering work, managing projects, developing and leading people, selling, and managing risk, but are now struggling to return to meaningful work simply because of a gap on their resumes.

Enter Emma. Prior to taking a three-year break, she had a varied career. She had a Master's degree in organizational psychology and had begun her career in HR before moving to a specialist management consulting firm, focusing on the programme management of large construction projects.

Her career took another twist when she was recruited to join the M&A team of a pan-European consulting firm.

Over her 15-year career, Emma had built up plenty of experience in leading people, developing teams, managing core business processes, and seeing major projects through to implementation — all valuable skills for a growing business like Wildsmith's.

Wildsmith hired Emma as Cutover's operations manager. He saved money by finding someone who wasn't at the executive level, and he saved time by finding someone with years of experience who didn't require much guidance. And he made another important step to ensuring the long-term success of his business. His team of 14 men had a woman on board. This was important to Wildsmith, he said, because "if everything goes to plan, I'm going to have to keep hiring. And some of the best candidates out there will be women. And if we don't have a woman on the team they won't even interview with us."

Emma was just the first. As the company continued to grow over the next few months, it needed talent to join in new roles in marketing and product development. Thinking creatively about where to look for new people and being excited about the prospect of building a properly diverse team, the leadership of Cutover added another 4 women to the team. They had no diversity programme, and indeed no head of HR. Each member of the leadership team was committed to having a balanced workforce. And everyone played a part in making that happen.

In a competitive environment with little spare time and cash, companies need to think creatively about where they find and how they deploy skilled people. The talent pool of returning women is an option companies can no longer afford to overlook.

SECTION
TWO

1

It begins in your head

Before you start searching the jobs pages, you probably need to do a little soul searching. Why? Because the stories we tell ourselves in our heads often stop us going back in a way that's as successful as it could be. At times, we create reasons, excuses – fallacies, if you like – that limit our expectations and ambitions. Whilst this might make life safe – there's less risk of failing if you don't set the bar too high – it also puts unnecessary boundaries around what YOU could achieve.

In this chapter we will:

- Introduce the concept of mental models – the assumptions we carry around in our heads about the way things are – and where they come from and suggest an exercise that will help you challenge your own.

- Explore some of the limiting beliefs – the stories we tell ourselves – that prevent us from returning to work, starting a new career or reigniting an old one.

- Introduce a tool – The Ladder of Inference – which will help you challenge your thinking and explore new possibilities.

MENTAL MODELS

Peter Senge, author of *The Fifth Discipline: The Art and Practice of the Learning Organisation*, would label such limiting beliefs 'Mental Models'. Mental models are the assumptions, stories, images and perspectives we carry in our minds. Assumptions about ourselves, other people, institutions, organisations, the world, effectively. Sometimes they're very helpful. They are an efficient way of helping us process large amounts of information very quickly.

The trouble is we often tell ourselves these stories as if they are absolutely true. As a result they can block progress. The key to unlocking these mental models is first to surface what they are and then to gather evidence to test whether they are true.

Here are some common fallacies – or mental models – that can get in the way of you returning to work. These are from our network and our research. The quotes in orange are from women (who had returned after a break) in response to our question "What would you say to others?"

"I'm needed at home. The family wouldn't cope without me." You've probably cast yourself in this role, becoming the default parent, making every job in the family your own, absorbing the domestic minutiae. Arguably this behaviour can come from a feeling of guilt about not working, or a need to feel indispensable. Division of labour and domestic tasks is always fraught but if you're clear and specific other people can do more.

> **"**Be kind to yourself. Put in place, accept and ask for help. Drop the desire for perfection. 80% is usually more than good enough and people on the receiving end don't notice the difference.**"**

"I'm unemployable. I've been out too long. My skills are not relevant." Common concerns. As if your earlier, often successful career counts for nothing. This is madness. Everything you learned and did before you took a career break did not suddenly get thrown out along with the disposable nappies. And what you've been doing during that break is additive. All that life experience enhances your ability to get a job done.

> **"**Believe in yourself. Remember you were great before and will add value. Keep learning, be interested. A career break brings new perspective and this is a hugely valuable asset. Fresh thinking, use it to your advantage.**"**

"I'm too old." Ageism is rife. And wrong. Don't become one of the perpetrators. You can't fix it overnight, but you can definitely fix how you respond. To other people's attitudes and comments and to your own perceptions, if they're holding you back. With age comes wisdom, perspective, experience. Some of the things you have done prior to your career break

– for example, dealing with challenges during the 2008/9 financial crisis – won't have been experienced by many in the market now.

"I've proved myself." Work is hard and the thought of mustering up the necessary drive, determination and energy, especially if you've already achieved in some shape or form, may not appear worth it. Working this through is very personal. For some people this may be right. For others, it can take deep reflection and other people's observations to help you understand how work can be part of achieving personal fulfilment.

> Annoushka Ducas took a break after she sold her business, Links of London in 2006. She never planned to return to this world but three years later, she was back, founding the eponymous jewellery brand Annoushka. It became clear to Annoushka and those around her that, creatively, she still had more in her. She has extraordinary energy and creative talent and was in no way ready for retirement. As well as running another highly successful business, she supports and mentors other women and is involved in Give a Future, a micro-finance programme based in Addis Ababa.

"The industry has moved on. I'm not up to speed with the trends." This is a fear of looking stupid. Break it down. Yes, things will have moved on. You need to be specific about how and find a way of plugging the gap. Many professions have industry bodies that can help. You will undoubtedly have friends who still work in your industry who can point you in the right direction. The chapter 'Wise Up' as some suggestions to help. Returnship programmes deliberately offer a significant amount of retraining.

"It's not worth it. The childcare costs will outweigh what I earn." There's a chapter dedicated to this particular fallacy, where we explain that you need to do a much longer-term equation to measure the financial impact of returning.

"I won't be as good as I was before." You'll be different. Possibly better. Jenni, whose story appears at the end of this chapter, was fearful that she couldn't be the teacher she once was, arriving at school at 7am and leaving after the caretaker. As it turned out, hours she worked was not the key to her success.

> **"**Don't assume that the break has rendered you unable to perform a job you once excelled at. It just doesn't. Don't apologies for your children but don't use them as an excuse to do less.**"**

"I'll be judged and found wanting." We've been there looking at our watches at 4.30pm when a member of the team has to leave early or won't be in on Friday because they work part-time. We've picked up their slack and begrudged them their 'privilege'.

This is probably going to happen at some point. Remember, you are there to do a job and should be judged on output. Being confident and clear about the value you're adding and being able to communicate that will be critical. We'll discuss this more in the chapter 'Staying Back'. Own your decisions. You have chosen not to work more hours than anyone else because you have other priorities as well. There is no shame in this.

> **"**Workaholics aren't heroes. They don't save the day, they just use it up.
> The real hero is home because she figured out a faster way to get things done.**"**
>
> Jason Fried & David Heinemeier Hansson, Rework

Hold out each assumption: be prepared to test it and find out just how true it really is.

Mental model	Evidence to prove this	The case against
The family couldn't cope without me being at home.	I do all the school runs, cook all the meals, open all the post, do all the admin. If I don't do it, it doesn't get done.	I've never actually asked anyone else to do any of this. Other people's kids take the bus to school. What did you do when stuff didn't get done?
I'm too old.	Everyone working there is a good 20 years younger than me. I'm too old to learn new methods & technologies.	Except the senior people who are about the same age as me. I taught myself how to use Hootsuite last weekend. It's an aging population.

I'm irrelevant, my skills are out of date.	It's all about digital marketing these days and I know nothing about that.	I understand the perspectives of female consumers very well – I am one. You are a consummate user of apps and platforms.
I couldn't go back at the same level because I need flexibility.	No-one in a senior position at my previous employer worked less than full time.	The Timewise Power 50 List has some pretty impressive people on it who have managed to negotiate flexible working arrangements. Did you ever ask?

What shapes our "mental models" of the world

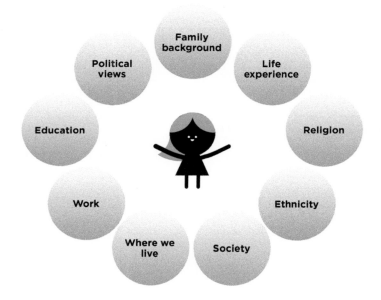

Our mental models are shaped by a variety of factors – our life experience to date, the way we've been brought up, our education, work experience, the community within which we live and many more.

They are deeply ingrained within us and often we hold them, unconsciously, as 'truths' about the way things are. And sometimes, to progress, to learn, to develop or to change things about our lives, we need to find a way to surface them, to challenge them and sometimes to reject them.

Your turn. Think about your own attitude and assumptions about returning to work, restarting your career or taking a new direction. Have a go at writing down the stories in your head that you're currently holding as truths. What evidence do you have that they are indeed true? Are there any hints that you could be wrong?

Think about your assumptions about:

- The role you could play
- The time required
- Financial requirements
- Who would value you
- What about the family?
- Your skill set
- Your capability
- Your age
- What would be expected of you

Read the limiting beliefs above – do any apply to you? Even if you're sure they're 'true', write them down. Find a trusted partner to discuss this with. Ask them to challenge you on the facts and evidence.

Mental model/ assumption	Evidence to prove this	The case against

THE LADDER OF INFERENCE

This second model is linked to the first. It's a tool to help you systematically process the way in which your mental models impact your decision making and actions.

It was first developed back in 1970 by American business theorist and Harvard professor Chris Argyris. Frankly, it's the best tool we have come across to help people slow down their thinking, question their assumptions and in doing so open themselves up to new possibilities.

The Ladder of Inference

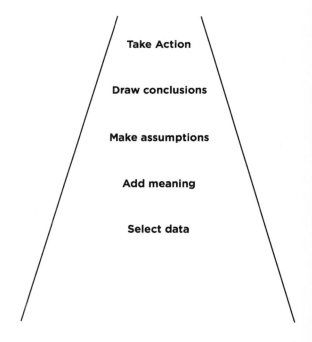

We were reminded of this tool when listening to the story of the magnificent Sandie Okoro, a lawyer who, at the time was senior vice-president and General Counsel of a global bank. She recounted the story of her approach when a promotion opportunity arose exactly at the time she found out she was pregnant.

Using the ladder of inference, here is the thinking and actions upon which she could very easily have landed.

1. She could have looked at her situation, her range of experience and the timing of the promotion opportunity (now), her pregnancy and **selected** some facts: the job was open now; she was pregnant.

2. **Adding meaning**: she was unsuitable for the job because she would be going off on maternity leave in 6 months.

3. She could have **made assumptions**: another good candidate would come along; her boss would not consider her for promotion given she had just announced her pregnancy. There was no way they would leave the job open for her. Negotiation wasn't an option.

4. This would lead to a **conclusion**: there would be little point applying.

5. The subsequent **action**: carry on in her current job and accept that the promotion opportunity was just at the wrong time.

The way anyone moves up their ladder of inference – from data to action – is driven by their mental models. In this case, assumptions about how a pregnant woman would be treated, the urgency and process used to fill a promotion vacancy, Sandie's own ability to negotiate and hustle.

The purpose of this tool is to help you slow down – identify where you're making assumptions – and question whether you are being blind to alternatives.

Sandie's mental models were quite different. She had a strong belief in herself and a view that it was up to her to negotiate, to hustle and to determine her future for herself. She also had a mental model that recruitment and selection processes in the bank were slow and cumbersome. And that her boss was relatively risk averse.

With that in mind, here is the story she told of the decisions and actions she took:

1. The **data**: She had a number of years in the role and her performance feedback was exceptional. Previous recruitment processes to find people at that level had taken over 4 months.

2. **Meaning:** She was an excellent candidate for the role and should at least apply.

3. **Assumptions:** Her boss was risk averse. She was a known quantity. If she could persuade him of her commitment he would at least consider her.

4. **Conclusion**: This is a role that is worth applying for. Demonstrate commitment and minimise the sense of disruption caused by maternity leave – comparing it to the length of the search process.

5. **Action:** Apply for the role, explain her commitment. Show maternity leave as a temporary blip that could easily be covered.

Sandie got the promotion and went on to greater things.

In another example, Alex (who we'll meet later in this book) knew when his wife was pregnant that he would have the opportunity to take six months shared parental leave.

He looked at that piece of data, added the picture he had in his mind of sleeping babies, concluded this was a good idea and took the time off, thinking:

"This will be great. Three months off work, being paid. Fabulous. Why wouldn't I."

Whilst he loved his experience, as most readers will know, his conclusion that this would be time 'off work' was fundamentally flawed. Whilst he loved his paternity leave, he would be the first to admit that his mental models about what being a parent of a young child entailed were somewhat misinformed.

In the *Fifth Discipline Fieldbook*, Rick Ross describes three steps when using mental models and the ladder of inference:

1. Become aware of your own thinking and assumptions and how they are driving your actions.

2. Articulate your reasoning and thinking.

3. Ask questions of others about their reasoning and conclusions.

WHAT'S GOING ON IN YOUR HEAD IS THE BIGGEST THING THAT WILL HOLD YOU BACK.

You have probably heard the anecdote about women only applying for jobs if they are 100% sure they can do everything on the job spec, whilst men think they'd be a perfect candidate if they can do 60% of what's there. Tara Sophia Mohr dug a little further into this for the *Harvard Business Review* . She found that it was pretty much true, for all sorts of reasons. Don't let this happen to you.

Recognise when you are making assumptions. Be prepared to test them. Be brave. Test them with someone else who can be objective. Think Nadia Hussein in the Great British Bake Off.

> **"**I am never ever going to put boundaries on myself again. I am never going to say I can't do it. I am never going to say I don't think I can. I can. And I will.**"**

Jenni's story

Jenni spent 12 years working as a teacher in large primary schools in economically deprived parts of inner city London. Tough gig. She loved it. More importantly, she was good at it. Pupils, parents, other teachers all told her so. Though, to be fair, she knew it herself.

A dedicated professional, she would be the first in school, arriving with the caretaker at 7am, and last to leave, well after 6pm. School holidays were spent planning and preparing for the forthcoming term.

There is a modern myth that teaching is an ideal job for someone with kids, but when Jenni had her own she found that this was far from the case. Her first didn't sleep well at all, her second wasn't much better, and she found herself unable to be the teacher she wanted to be at the same time as coping as the mother of two very small, very demanding, very needy human beings. So she quit.

After a break of over 10 years, and now approaching 40, Jenni decided it was time to return.

Having accepted the time was right and that family life was perhaps not so dependent on her, Jenni then had to confront an even more frightening prospect. Being past it.

"I was a chalk and talk teacher," she told me. "People don't think of teaching as being particularly high tech, but we're using technology all the time and I had no idea where to start. On top of which, every new education secretary changes something, and there have been at least 5 of them since I left, plus I felt old and irrelevant. And even though my kids were older, there was still no way I could be the sort of teacher I used to be, in at the crack of dawn and there till the lights were turned off. I also wanted to do four days a week, which is pretty unheard of for a primary school classroom teacher."

Armed with a growing conviction that returning to work was really important to her, Jenni made a plan. She took a short course on special needs education, which reminded her that she actually did already know lots about teaching; talked to other teachers working at local schools; used her network to let people know she was coming back; and let her family know exactly what it was going to mean for them.

"The first three months, I was on my knees," she recalled. "I had so much to learn. I took the tech support guy a cake and persuaded him to give me half-an-hour a week on things like how the electronic whiteboard worked. I took a lesson for another teacher in return for her bringing me up to speed on a new part of the curriculum. And I couldn't have done without a very supportive husband. For those three months, the kids knew that I couldn't be the first call they made in a crisis. It had to be him. And they helped, even down to helping me prep materials for some of my lessons over the weekend."

What is more revealing, though, is to hear Jenni talk now, three years on, about the sort of teacher she is today.

"One of the things stopping me was a fear that I wouldn't be able to be the teacher I was before. And I'm not. But I think I'm actually better. I was worried about being too old. Irrelevant. I was so used to thinking of myself as 'just a mum', that I forgot about all the things I did when I wasn't working that I now bring to the classroom and that make me better."

As well as training as a Samaritan and working for a homeless charity, Jenni was chair of trustees of a large, charitable nursery company. When it went into financial distress, she orchestrated the buy-out and sale to another company, saving the livelihoods of many people in the process.

"My people skills are so much stronger than when I was in my twenties. And I can relate to the parents so much more. I teach children with special needs; their parents are often worried and they trust what I have to say. I don't work the long hours anymore and you know what, I don't need to. I'm so much more effective. I am so glad to be working again."

What advice would Jenni give?

"Don't tell yourself you're unemployable. I'm amazed at how women who've spent time off are so quick to write off everything they did before they took a break. It's still there. It's not as if being a mother writes all of that off. You're actually adding to your skills if anything, not taking them away. And yes, you might not go back to doing the work you did before in the same way you did it before, but you might actually find you're so much better than before."

Our original inspiration for this book was to support women returning after a career break. The more people we talked to, the more we realised the messages are relevant to a wider audience. To women who have taken their foot off the gas for a while, but who deep down are not done with career ambition. Women – and men – who find themselves in the wrong role and want to take a different path, if only they knew how.

The need to look deep inside your own head is an important first step whatever your situation.

Mel Eusebe brought this message home to us when we talked to her for one of the early chapters. Her story shows how easy it is for each of us to lose sight of the end goal; to let time fly by; to find ourselves with work that doesn't somehow feel worth the sacrifices we're making.

Melanie Eusebe's story

Mel had always wanted to be an entrepreneur. She joined EY because she'd seen others train there and go on to set up their own businesses. 17 years later she was still there; now a highly successful financial services strategy consultant. Well paid and well respected. Not an entrepreneur.

The 'whack on the head' came when Mel read *Your Money or Your Life*, by Vicki Robin and Joe Dominguez. In one chapter the book asks readers to think about what they are spending and question whether it merits the hours required to earn the necessary funds. Mel realised that not only was the designer handbag not worth the effort, the rest of her work didn't feel meaningful enough either.

"What I wish looking back," she told us, "was that someone had told me about time. How fast it goes. I realised I'd missed out on having children; I was spending my life on planes; I'd lost sight of my goal."

Some people in this situation find reasons to carry on: the mortgage, a lifestyle, comfort; why take a risk? Mel, by her own admission, spent a long time exploring what was going on in her head. And decided she had to make a change. She cut back on her lifestyle in order to prepare herself to take a big risk.

"I decided that if I had sacrificed having kids, then I at least had to give birth to something," she explained. "My work had to leave a legacy for someone."

Mel's immediate legacy is the Black British Business Awards, the only the only premium awards programme that recognises, rewards and celebrates exceptional performance and achievements of black people in businesses operating in Great Britain. And that was just the beginning.

Your Checklist for this Chapter

✓ What's stopping you?

✓ Have you taken time to think about everything you perceive as a barrier to your return, real or imagined?

✓ Have you tested these barriers with others or with a tried and tested model?

✓ Are you ready in your head?

Other Resources

The Fifth Discipline: The Art and Practice of the Learning Organisation by Peter Senge

Free! Love Your Work, Love Your Life by Chris Barez-Brown

Your Money or Your Life, by Vicki Robin and Joe Dominguez

It's Not How Good You Are It's How Good You Want to Be by Paul Arden

2.

Getting your story straight

"Stories are data with soul.**"**
Brene Brown US author, speaker and scholar

Let's assume there's a chance you didn't read our piece Play the Long Game in Chapter 2.

when you were 22. Let's instead imagine you're sitting there at 35, or 45 or even 55, with previous experience of work, maybe even a post grad qualification of some sort; ambitions to return to work in some shape or another; and a worrying gap on your CV. Where do you start?

Ultimately, you're going to need a story. A narrative. Your best chances of returning to do something that you're going to love are being clear what that is and then harnessing the powers of your network – more on this later – to help you make connections, get interviews and then land that job.

The Americans (and lots of sales people) call this an 'Elevator Pitch'. Others talk about thinking of yourself as 'A Brand Called You'. As Jeff Bezos, founder of Amazon put it:

> **"**Your brand is what people say about you when you're not in the room.**"**

But never mind about all of that right now. Just think about it as being your story.

It needs to be short enough and memorable enough for someone else to use it to help connect you with people who could help you get a meeting, a connection, an opening an ultimately a job.

Some examples:

"You must meet Carol. She had twenty years' experience doing PR and crisis management in the city and left around 10 years ago when she and her partner made a lifestyle decision to move to the country. She's passionate about improving social care and would love to use her PR and comms skills in that sector."

"Sally was a bit of a rebel and left school at 16 to travel the world. She ended up living in New Zealand and the Far East before settling in Italy for 8 years. Returning to the UK, she got a job as a production assistant at Sky Sports, before taking time off to bring up her children. She's recently helped to run and then sell a family company and has managed a couple of building projects. She's got really strong admin skills and is looking for a role as an office manager, ideally for a services business that deals with the creative sector."

"Lola spent 12 years in branding and marketing for an asset management company. She's taken a couple of years off whilst her daughter was very young but now wants to get back. She's really interested in small, growing businesses, and is looking for an opportunity to take on a wider marketing role for companies in that sector."

"I have to introduce you to Ameena. She's a communications expert who has worked in corporate affairs, PR and investor relations for multi-national industrial products companies. She has a lot of experience dealing with Government and regulatory bodies, particularly in Asia and is keen to support tech scale ups who are now looking to expand into those markets."

"When she graduated, Abi joined a fledgling radio station that grew rapidly to become one of the biggest independents in the country. She was creative director when she left to take a break. She's always been passionate about netball and has remained heavily involved as a coach with a semi-professional team. She is looking to return to a creative, sales & marketing or business development role with a female sporting body or organisation."

Those stories might look succinct and simple, but believe us they didn't start out that way. We've seen CVs that run to 6 pages – no wonder when we are dealing with women who might have had a 20-year career and a 10-year career gap during which few of them will have been sitting at home all day.

So how do you get to something this simple and straightforward?

For women like us, there are a number of elements that could make up this story:

- Your strengths, your talents
- Your professional experience and background
- What you're interested in
- What you've been up to since you left (if indeed you did leave)
- How that all translates to what you want to do next

Consider a career coach

Don't worry about getting the lines right straight away. Begin with an open mind. The right coach can be invaluable: Someone who is skilled, to help deepen your thinking, who will ask you questions that you might shy away from and provide you with time to think deeply about your future.

> "Hannah Rix, my career coach went through a very rigorous and energising process that matches my skillset, values and ambitions, which then gave me a framework from which to shortlist career and business ideas. The sessions helped me to focus and develop a plan of action that was relevant, new, creative and more dynamic."
> Diane Schaefer

We'd encourage you to consider finding a great coach, one who is professionally qualified and comes personally recommended. Someone who can guide you through a structured process. Yes, it costs, but how often do you think twice about spending money on others? Maybe now is the time to invest in your own professional development.

Mentors can also be useful – having people around you to guide and advise. We've been lucky enough to work with many, including Averil Leimon, founder of the White Water Group and author of several books on business and performance coaching. Averil provided excellent insights into the specific challenges women face in their career and the ways in which coaching can help.

Our intention is not to replace the expertise of a one to one coach but to provide some questions to stimulate your thoughts and exercises to kickstart your journey.

1. Mapping your career journey

Find a large sheet of paper and turn it to landscape. A4 will do, A3 better, a flip chart even better. Plot your career journey from start to today.

Think about how you got to where you are today. Was it a straight path or were there some odd detours, some major breakdowns, road crashes, major stalls?

Here's a couple of simple examples – yours could be much more elaborate:

CAREER ATTAINMENT

AGE

22   32   42

Grad programme
Recession
Secondment to News Corp
Promoted to senior mgr
Personal life in crisis
Moved jobs
Maternity leave 1
Back to work struggle
Maternity leave 2 and mum ill
Part-time role
Resigned

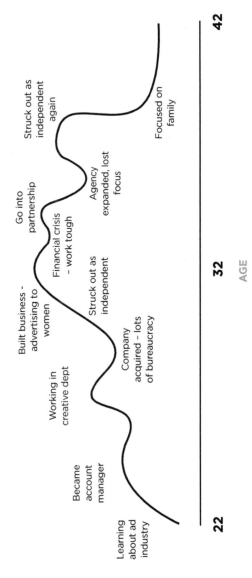

CAREER ATTAINMENT

AGE

22

32

42

Learning about ad industry

Became account manager

Working in creative dept

Built business - advertising to women

Company acquired - lots of bureaucracy

Struck out as independent

Go into partnership

Financial crisis - work tough

Agency expanded, lost focus

Struck out as independent again

Focused on family

- Now put in all the key turning points/decision points along the way.

- Notice where you had choice points and might have ended up somewhere else. Draw in some of the side roads – where might they have taken you?

- What do you notice about the highs and lows? What were the high points? Where did you have the greatest sense of achievement? Where were you at your happiest?

- Break the diagram up into chunks of time that make sense for you – around 3 – 5 years. For each section, jot down what you were most proud of.

Step back and look for common themes.

To get the most out of this exercise, try to do it with a trusted friend and when you have time and space for proper reflection.

2. Identify your strengths, your talents

Think about the career journey you've drawn and reflect on those highlights. What was it that gave you energy? Then think about what strengths you were drawing on then. Ask other people for help and insight.

When I was at my best	What was my impact/ role/ contribution	What strength or talent was I using?

Think back to your performance reviews at work. What do they tell you about your strengths?

> **"**I kept my performance reviews and re-read them to remind myself of what I was capable of before my world turned into nappies and feeds. It really helped me in feeling confident about my professional capabilities when I had to redo my CV.**"**
> Survey respondent

It's also worth thinking about external factors too. Are you most comfortable working independently or in a team? Do you thrive when there is structure or prefer ambiguity? Do you enjoy a corporate environment, or does it bring you out in a rash?

Do the same exercise but with an external lens.

When I was at my best	What sort of people was I working with?	What environment was I working in?

There are also plenty of online resources to help with this sort of exercise, such as Gallup's *Strength Finder*, now called Clifton Strengths.

Compare the two. Establish what feels right for you. Ask your partner, friends, colleagues if this resonates with them. Are you missing anything?

This helps you establish, from everything you've done and experienced, what are your real strengths. We are all much happier and much more successful when we play to our strengths so that's a good place to start when thinking about what you want to do next.

3. Your professional skills and experience.

The bit you've forgotten. Everything that many women think went out in the bin along with the disposable nappies.

However long your break, the likelihood is that before it you were a very capable, successful professional. Even if you didn't see yourself that way – and we know how good women are at adopting imposter syndrome.

All of this hasn't gone away and you need to capture it. Most importantly, you need to be ready to recite it in a way which is going to impress people. This will feel odd. It will feel as though you are boasting about yourself. How ridiculous is it that we're very happy to talk about our children's achievements, or how amazing our friends are at what they do, or even (sometimes) our partners? The fact is we're not great at bigging up ourselves. Big mistake.

Everyone's experience is different but try these questions as a way of capturing your professional skills and experience in a memorable way. Remember, we're creating a story here.

- What have you studied?

- What professional qualifications do you have?
- What industries have you worked in?
- What sort of organisations have you worked for? Large, small, public, private, not for profit?
- What phases or an organisation's life have you experienced – start up, expansion, merger, acquisition, sale, insolvency, buy-out?
- What languages do you speak?
- What major projects have you delivered?
- What processes or technologies are you an expert in?

Now put those together in a STORY. Facts tell. Stories sell.

Here's what Lisa's succinct story might look like.

"Lisa had a 20-year career in management consulting, where she specialised in leadership and change management in the media sector. She then moved to become Director of Brand at Deloitte where she led a project to secure the firm's sponsorship of the London 2012 Olympics."

Now, to be perfectly honest, Lisa never saw herself as being a very good management consultant, and as well as media companies she dabbled a bit in FMCG. And for 2 of the 20 years was working in audit, and for 4 of the 20 years she would probably tell you she was most likely doing a bit of internal work, working on bids, going on holiday, faffing around. And that Olympic bid – well, it was a big team, and we were tier 2 sponsors not tier 1 ...... Who cares??

The point is to create a story about yourself that someone

else will be able to remember and connect with. We would always advocate being authentic but beware the tendency which women have to equivocate, put caveats around everything and generally put themselves down. Now is not the time to be self-effacing.

4. **Step 4 is then to think about what you're interested in.**

What do you really enjoy? Don't worry about whether there is a career here, or even a link to your strengths. Just try to think freely about what you love. Where do you spend your time, given a choice?

Zoe Cunningham, author of *Networking Know-How: connecting for success* recommends using a word cloud. Brainstorm a list of 50 words that reflect your interests, your personality or your passions.

Another approach is to ask yourself some very specific questions:

1. What do you love learning about? What gives you a buzz and leaves you wanting to know more?

2. What activities or experiences leave you feeling fully engaged? When does time fly?
    When you're passionate about something, often it feels like time has ceased to exist.

3. What activities or experiences make you feel alive?
    Think of as many as you can. Things that make you feel good about yourself. Activities that give you a sense of achievement and serenity at the same time.

4. What sort of things do people regularly ask your advice and opinion on? When you're passionate about something you're often seen by others as an expert, even though it might not feel that way to you.

5. If money were no object and you knew you had another 100 years to live, what would you love to be doing?   What would keep you stimulated, happy and fulfilled?

By asking these questions, you should be able to identify some common themes that help draw out what you're really interested in. Don't be judgemental with yourself. It's more important to be honest than to impress someone else.

5. Mind the gap

If you're reading this book, the likelihood is you've had a career gap of some sort. There are two schools of thought here. One is that you should treat it like the war, politics and religion – don't mention it. The other is the opposite.

Given that one of our beliefs is that what you do outside of work makes you *more* effective in work, you can guess which side we come down on.

In her recent book *How Hard Can it Be*, the author and journalist Allison Pearson writes a very funny chapter on how the protagonist has to extract activities she carried out as a mother to make up credible roles for her CV.

"Time management and prioritisation: I have balanced the complex needs of different individuals and developed routines while learning to prioritise multiple tasks and meet strict deadlines". And "Provided sustainable nutritional support for staff in line with industry standards... (always kept snacks for kids...)."

The things you've been doing outside work have **added** to your previous skills and experience. You need to think hard about what they are and what extra value they have added to you as a potential employee.

Here are some examples. Add your own.

Activity	Value
Trained as a Samaritan	Listening skills, empathy, counselling
Trustee of a charity	Legal requirements, financial responsibilty, planning, compliance
Renovating a building	Project management, dealing with suppliers, negotiation
Being a magistrate	Judgement, understanding of the law, team working, understanding local culture
Set up small business	Innovating, selling, business acumen, getting things done

Your experience in your gap may or may not feed directly into the story about you – who you are, what you're interested in and what you want to do next – but it will inevitably be useful when it comes to your CV, your Linked In profile and the interview you succeed in getting.

As John Purkiss and David Royston-Lee write in their brilliant book *Brand You*:

Facts tell. Stories Sell.

So now you need to do the really hard work of drawing this all together and creating your short, memorable story. The few sentences that tell people who you are, what you care about and that link to what you want to do next.

Like the ones at the top of this chapter. The elevator pitch. Your brand. What someone will say about you when you're not in the room.

Given the breadth of your experience to date, it's highly likely that you will come up with a number of alternatives. That's fine. Draw up a long list and then hone it to a short list. In her book *Working Identity: Unconventional Strategies for Reinventing Your Career*, Herminia Ibarra provides advice for mid-career professionals who are reevaluating their career paths and their futures. She advocates beginning with a long list of what she describes as "possible future selves".

Returning to Lisa, looking to return after an 8-year break from a career as a consultant and Director of Brand and Communications, here's what her long list might have looked like:

1. Build on my marketing and communications background and consult to small, growing businesses in the local area.

2. Return to work as a management consultant specialising in retention of women.

3. Take a leap from voluntary work as a magistrate and retrain in law. Consider specialising in employment law and equality.

4. Move on from blogging. Become a writer professionally. Take a course on business journalism.

5. Set up a business to shine a light on the issues faced by women who've taken a career break and want to return.

You might land on your ideal future very quickly. Or it might take some time. In later chapters we will touch on the things you can do to explore possible alternatives. The point of this chapter, though, is to help you articulate at least one option in an elevator pitch so that you are well positioned to find the help you need.

And here's the really frightening thing. Once you've done that, you need to hone it down to a 5 second pitch. In case the elevator's only going up one floor.

Carol's a PR and comms expert for companies delivering social care.

Sally is an office manager for support services to creatives.

Lola helps SMEs get their branding and marketing activities right.

Ameena advises tech companies on PR and comms to support their global expansion.

Abi's a creative director with a passion for netball.

Get it?

Off you go.

Your Checklist for this Chapter

✓ Have you taken a step back and mapped out your career journey to date?

✓ Can you say what your key strengths and talents are?

✓ Do you have a succinct story about your professional qualifications and experience, that isn't a long list?

✓ Do you know what you're really interested in?

✓ Are you able to articulate how what you did in your break adds to your value?

✓ Have you taken time to combine this information into a coherent narrative?

✓ Have you considered investing in a recommended, suitably qualified career coach who can help?

Other Resources

Working Identity: Unconventional strategies for reinventing your career by Herminia Ibarra

StrengthsFinder 2.0 by Tim Rath

Playing Big: Find your voice, your vision and make things happen by Tara Mohr

Brand You: Turn your unique talents into a winning formula by John Purkiss and David Royston-Lee

Time to Think: Listening to ignite the human mind by Nancy Kline

3

It's not what you know ... the power of the network

We recently described *This Mum Runs* as a fabulous example of a network.

> "Is this a network? I thought of it more as a really supportive community," was a common response.

With roots in Bristol, this community began when founder, Mel Bound, had the idea that mothers stuck at home, feeling isolated, would benefit from time outside, doing exercise with other women in the same situation.

Is this a network in the purest sense? Absolutely. It's an incredibly supportive and nurturing community. That's **exactly** what we mean by a network.

A Mindset Shift

Networking - the "Old"	Networking – the "New"
• Old boys	• Interesting people
• Selling	• Helping
• Competitive, sharp elbows	• Supportive
• Stuffy hotel rooms	• Part of daily life
• Buisness cards	• Contact details
• Warm chardonnay	• Good coffee, chilled wine
• "I know no-one"	• (S)he was great
• Get me out of here	• Let's meet again
• What can I get?	• Small strokes, little and often
	• Online
	• What can I give?

This chapter explains:

● Why networks are so important

● Fundamental principles that underpin great networking

● How to build your network

WHY ARE NETWORKS SO IMPORTANT?

#karmanotkickbacks

We love this hashtag, shared by the brilliant Amelia Torode, Founder of The Fawnbrake Collective, an agile network of brand strategists. It neatly sums up our perspective on networking. And yet we know so many people dread the thought of networking events. Evenings spent in hotel meeting rooms, enforced conviviality, sipping warm white wine, making small talk with people you've never met before.

Hold that thought – and be prepared to change it. Our research found that if you're returning to work, you are 4 times more likely to find a job though your network than you are through a recruitment agency. Starting a business, changing your career, raising money for charity, writing a book, looking for some creative inspiration, bringing value back to your business...you name it, lots of things are far more likely to be successful if you have the right network. And network with purpose.

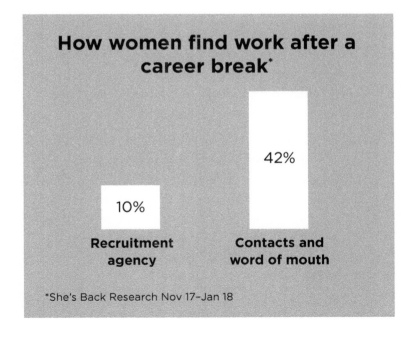

How women find work after a career break*

10% — Recruitment agency

42% — Contacts and word of mouth

*She's Back Research Nov 17–Jan 18

Accelerating your career or finding work from a standing start can be isolated and isolating. Having a tribe who empathise and actively want you to succeed can be an emotional lifeline. They've got your back, they say good luck and cheer your successes.

The building industry remains male dominated. – women we interviewed for this book speak of frequently being the sole female on site. Lonely, zero fun and frequently very macho. A group of women from that sector decided it was time to do something different. By building a network. Here's their incredible story.

How women in building took on the men at their own game

Club Peloton is a building industry networking and fundraising charity which raises money through long distance, grueling cycle rides. It's predominantly male. Understandable given the sector and the activity.

Jennifer Ross and Claire Treanor had been members for some time and were struck by the way in which the men involved gained huge benefits. Determined to reap some of those benefits for themselves and for other women, they founded VeloCity. They convinced 25 women to join them on a charity ride from London to Paris. Now an annual event, VeloCity's long-distance rides raise significant sums for charity.

As the two of them suspected, pushing yourself to the limits of your endurance is a great way to form strong bonds.

"When you've been there suffering frostbite, accidents and awful weather and you still have 80 miles to go, you really do pull together as a team," explained Jennifer.

Some of the women involved decided to put these bonds to good use and agreed to look out for an opportunity to work together on a commercial project. Eventually they spotted one – the complex and highly prestigious National Infrastructure Commission ideas competition to submit proposals for redevelopment of a swathe of land between Oxford and Cambridge. The challenge was how to provide homes and transport for a million more people without at the same time destroying large parts of the countryside.

"It gave us an idea to explore all the things we talked about on the bike to do with making great places, so we thought why not!"

As a group they visited Rotterdam and Amsterdam and examined long-term government-led planning objectives, new towns and housing extensions, fostering debate between each other. They also continued to cycle together, talking through their ideas, enjoying the growing camaraderie and above all having fun.

They were competing against 54 entries. They were decidedly the underdogs. Working outside of their already existing intense professional and family commitments (most of them are mums), the team were spurred on by the fresh idea of an all-female planning/architect/ engineering consortium.

Since they were a newly formed consortium, they had no formal process to fall back on; no pre-existing assumptions about any element of their proposal. They thought laterally, took on board ideas from all sorts of different sources, put health and wellbeing at the heart, challenged each other to be creative and forward thinking. Bikes were at the centre of the proposal of course, with existing B roads being used to form cycle and walking routes.

On 5th December 2017 it was announced that the team's entry, VeloCity had won, beating large-scale, well-established global practices.

What had they learned? That informal associations of professionals can be highly effective, creative and mutually supportive. That joint challenges really do develop trust. They hope to use this initial success to continue to generate further new ideas and thinking.

"I guess it endorses that out of taking part in something great things grow out of such events. I think it is up to us to spread the word and give support to lots of women doing their thing their way."

NETWORKING FUNDAMENTALS

Building a great network is going to be an important part of your search for work. Perhaps *the* most important part. The good news is, it's a bit like learning to ride a bike: a bit uncomfortable at first but once you master it, it becomes second nature. Here are some handy hints. Above all, networking is all about finding lots of people you can help.

Yes, you read that correctly. People YOU can help, not the other way around. That's Rule Number 1. There are a few more too. Here they are:

Networking is an Act of Generosity

> **"**The currency of real networking is not greed but generosity.**"**
> Keith Ferrazzi Never Eat Alone

Be interested in people and curious to find out how you might be able to help them. What are their personal and professional challenges? Whether you're meeting people at work, at an event, at the school gates, wherever, discover connections and figure out where and how you can help. It could be small – recommend a book, a post, an event, or introduce them to someone. Just try to help, if not immediately, at some point in the future.

This means asking questions and listening to the answers. Focus on being interested, not interesting. A subtle but important shift. Helping people, being genuinely interested in them, will help form connections that are the bedrock of great relationships.

> **"**You can make more friends in two months by becoming interested in other people, than you can in two years by trying to get other people interested in you.**"**
> Dale Carnegie How to win friends and influence people

You are not your job (or nobody puts Lisa in the corner...)

Lisa had left a great job with an impressive sounding title and was now a full-time mum. She found herself at a charity dinner in between two men she didn't know.

When asked her the dreaded question – what do you do – Lisa felt woefully unprepared, flummoxed even, responding rather apologetically – well I used to be...

Lisa isn't alone. She made the all too common mistake of colluding in the frankly mad theory that our current professional role equals with our value. She ignored all the other things she had to offer for discussion; 20 years' experience of working life, bringing up children, the books she'd read, hobbies, passions, interests.

Feeling pretty diminished and not too great about herself, Lisa planned her responses for her next social event – and had a robust discussion about the challenges of women in the workplace and what their respective organisations were doing.

Lisa hasn't lost her brain, her point of view or her value. Plan your responses, don't talk about what you did – yes, it's important but what skills did the role give you, what are you planning to do now, what are you involved in, what do you have views on? Have those responses off pat.

It's a truth universally acknowledged ...That like all great novels you need a great opening line.

You need a few. You need some questions to open:

"What brings you here?"

"What did you think of the speakers?"

"How did you find the exhibition?"

That's the easy bit.

You also need some opening lines about yourself, ideally that don't rely on you having one of those high-status job titles that, while confidence boosting, can actually be a bit of a turn off if what you're trying to do is connect with the other person.

Networking is all about people. People don't want to hear about what you do – even though that's sometimes their default opening line – they're much more interested in who you are. This has to be authentic and should be about the *whole you*, not simply the role you play at work. It should give people an idea of what you're bringing to the party and what you're hoping to achieve. It will take time to craft and you should probably test on a few people before you play it for real.

This might include your elevator pitch (see chapter 2 in this section); but even if you haven't honed that yet you still need something to say.

HOW TO BUILD YOUR NETWORK IN REAL LIFE

You may feel your network lacks numbers or is of limited value when it comes to getting work or changing direction.

The well-known theory 'six degrees of separation' means that within 6 moves you can use your contacts to get to anyone in the world. Sounds improbable but it's a tested hypothesis and we've seen it play out successfully several times.

Deb has a background in theatre and education and now works with companies guiding their teams to deliver great presentations in competitive situations. (She does an awful lot of other things but that's one of her 'elevator pitches'). She happened to be having a cup of tea with a builder who was doing work for her a few years ago and they got talking about what she did. A few weeks later she took a call from a small firm of architects with an imminent critical pitch – they were in the final, known as the underdogs, needed help. She now has an impressive list of architect clients, large and small, and has helped them win many very large scale international projects.

Lisa was far from having her story straight a few years ago but was talking to a local florist, who she'd got to know over the years. When Theo asked her how things were going, she mentioned her idea for She's Back and he told her about two friends, Nikki and Katherine, who he sensed might be doing something similar. Called Digital Mums. Over the years we've pointed a large number of women in their direction and they have been super supportive of our work, helping build our online networks and sharing our research.

Coincidences – not so. Both Lisa and Deb were unafraid to share what they did in language that made sense. That encouraged others to tell others. Deb built her business through word of mouth – she wasn't afraid to ask people if they knew someone who could use her skills. Advocacy remains the most powerful marketing strategy. So, think strategically.

Surfacing and mobilising your existing network

For this to work for you, you need to be systematic about first surfacing your network then putting it to work for you.

Think broadly – how and when do – or did you – come into contact with other people?

Here are some ideas from our world:

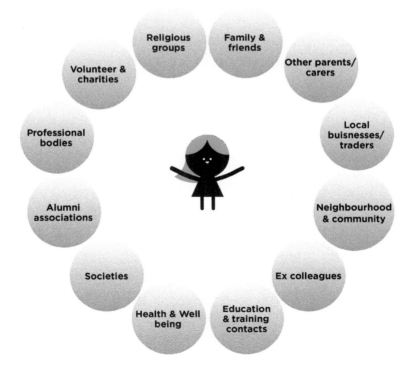

For example:

- Education and training: have you taken any courses recently? Do you have a list of other attendees? Are you in touch with university or college alumni associations or groups?
- Professional bodies: do you have a professional qualification? Does your professional body have an advocacy or support group? Are you signed up to all of their communications?
- Health and well-being: who do you meet at the gym? At yoga? On the touchline watching kids play sport? Walking the dog?
- Volunteers and charities: who else is involved? Do you know what else they get up to outside of this role? Shared values are often a strong way in with people.
- Other parents: We tend to know them as "Mum of ..." or "Dad of ..." or "looking after ..." but do you know anything else about them? What are they interested and involved in? Where do they work?
- Neighbourhood/community: who do you say hello to? Who have you been involved in initiatives or local events with? E.g. a group who got together to lobby on the council on parking? A group who organise a street party?

Think laterally about all the people you come into contact with and then have a systematic approach to working out how to capitalise on your existing network.

Stage one hopefully generated a large list. Now's the time to hone it so that you can target your efforts. Who are you going to approach first and why? Tip: keep it manageable. Choose 20 maximum. Think about:

- How could your skills or experience be relevant or helpful to them? Don't worry if it feels a bit remote at this point.

- How relevant is their position or experience to what you're trying to do?

- How easy will it be to have an honest conversation about what you're trying to achieve?

Here's an example, taking parents from the school gate when Lisa was first setting up She's Back

Name	What do they do?	Where's the connection?	How can I help
Christina	Chief Technology Office at FT	She's a senior woman in tech – v unusual. Would love to get her views on the issues. Might she spread word on our research?	She's about to change roles – I know several people in new place – could I help with intros?
Sonja	Runs nursery	Knows all about the trials & tribulations of working women, especially cost of childcare. Likely to be supportive of our cause.	Regularly help each other out with school stuff.
Chan	Has own contract cleaning business	Successfully juggling career & 3 kids – how?? She could help share research survey with her network.	I can send new clients her way.

Derrick	HR Director at News UK	He sees what's happening to his wife – who's taken a break from consulting career – and the women in his company. Looking for any advice and willing to make intros to journalists.	Wonder if his wife is ready to do a bit of freelance work? Could do with the help.
Sally	Full time mum	Wants to go back to work. Would love any help we can provide. Has large network of other mums to share survey.	Can provide lots of advice and contacts to support her own return.

We're completing this table retrospectively and on day one many of the boxes would have been blank. It's your job now to create a table for yourself and make a plan. It might not be a table, but do something that uses a systematic process, removes the emotion and enables you to track and measure progress. Which will be encouraging.

The key steps are:

1.   Identify who could be an ally.

2.   What do you know already and where are the gaps?

3.   How could you be helpful to them.

4.   Do they know what you're looking for? Have you delivered your elevator pitch?

5.   Could they possibly be helpful to you?

You'll be surprised what gems come out of simply taking a different look at the people you already know.

A word of caution

We're not talking about flooding your social acquaintances with business cards or bombarding them with a sales pitch about your future career. You're reasonably old and wise. Capitalise on your attuned social skills and emotional intelligence. Be sensitive. Be alert.

Can I buy you a coffee to ask your advice?

It might not be a coffee, it might be a walk in the park, a glass of wine, a chat at the school gates. Mobilising your existing network is largely about finding time to talk to them. To work out how you can help them and how they can help you. People are generally flattered and want to help. Ask them when would suit them or when would work. Take their lead, minimise admin and make it easy for them. Be open-minded, keep connections in mind and be prepared to be amazed where things lead.

If your experience is anything like ours, you will inevitably go down some blind alleys. Don't be discouraged. As Deb likes to say, "you have to be prepared to kiss a lot of frogs."

HOW TO GROW YOUR NETWORK

This also means meeting new people and there are myriad of ways of doing that. There are so many people out there who share your skills and interests, who meet up on a regular basis and help to connect people. Dive in – they will almost certainly welcome you with open arms.

Most people begin this online. It's never been easier to find and connect with people who have similar interests. Facebook groups and LinkedIn groups are the most obvious and widely used and many groups and associations have an online portal for members.

Examples include:

- Alumni organisations: does an old employer organise regular events for alumni? Even if you're not looking to return there, they can be a great way of catching up with ex-colleagues.

- Professional bodies: the ICAEW for accountants, MCA for consultants, the Law Society, the Institute of Civil Engineers, RIBA – most of these professional bodies have someone tasked with keeping and accelerating more women in the profession, refreshing professional skills and, often, returning to work.

- Business associations: the British Chambers of Commerce, Scottish Enterprise, the CBI are all worth a look. The BCC for example, operate in 52 towns or cities and some regularly offer workshops for people returning after a break.

- Online communities such as *We Are the City*, whose mission is "to support the female pipeline", offer free access to a myriad of resources such as women's networks, training, events and conferences. We Are the City also has a job board, a careers club plus host several awards throughout the year to showcase the female talent pipeline.

- Locally organised groups such as *Mummy's Gin Fund*, which currently covers London and the South East, provide resources, support, connections and a sense of community for their members.

- Professional advocacy groups such as Women in Film & TV, Women in Tech groups, Women in Journalism and She Says who are the only global networking organization for women in the creative industry and offer free mentorship and events in over 16 cities worldwide.
- Specialist recruiters who often run face to face events to upskill potential candidate base.
- Women in ... Organisations. Pretty much every sector we've come across has one and often they exist in different locations around the country.
- Lean In Circles Inspired by the phenomenal success of Sheryl Sandberg's book of the same name, these are small groups who meet regularly to learn and grow together. There are currently 34,000 groups in over 150 countries and its network is growing all the time.

These groups inspire and guide – a wonderful thing to behold. There are people like you who crave a sense of community, to belong to a tribe and a place to connect with like-minded souls.

We spoke to Vanessa Vallely, founder of We Are the City, for her top tips on building relationships (she, too eschews the word networking).

"Always start out with what you can do for others as opposed to what they can do for you. Build trust, build rapport, do what you say you are going to do and doors of opportunity will start to open. Remember to pay it forward, always help others along the way and never discard a contact. Keep in touch and above all, keep your relationships warm."

If you can't find a network that works for you, think about setting one up.

Ruth Cherry, Founder, Leeds Leans In

Ruth was a diligent attendee at local women's networking events. Asking around, the general consensus was that these large events, whilst well meaning, were of little practical use for the local female corporate finance and banking community which remains very male dominated, particularly in the PE and advisory firms. The women's events lacked the targeted opportunities Ruth and her colleagues were looking for.

Ruth started a monthly Lean In circle. The aim is to nurture a mutually supportive network with some focus and structure. She draws on resources on the Lean In website designed to support groups dealing with issues such as being more ambitious at work, negotiating work life balance, dealing with sexual harassment, negotiating for better pay and conditions.

Leeds Leans In now has 20-plus members working across legal, advisory, consultancy, transaction support and private equity.

"I've been quite cheeky in asking the larger employers who have members in the group to support us in offering space and the occasional sandwich."

As well as being of immediate and practical use today, it will undoubtedly prove useful as their careers progress.

Create your own plan for developing your network. This table is a suggested starting point.

Area of my life	Potential network	Action
Professional qualification (e.g. accountant)		
Alumni organisation		
Women in ...		
Music/drama/the arts		
Local business community		
Charitable sector		
Volunteer groups		
Sport/leisure/cultural activity		

Networking Events & Conferences

There are books dedicated to this stuff, which we don't propose to rewrite – the Other Resources chapter in Section 3 has some recommendations. Instead, we'll share some ways we manage to get through them without losing the will to live:

1. Do your research. Who's going to be there? What topics are going to be covered? What's your view? What information do you have to add?

2. Know your targets. Don't be shy about approaching them – politely. They are there to network too.

3. Breaks are where the real work happens. Don't hide in the toilets or bury yourself in the conference paperwork. Grab a coffee, breathe out go and chat to people

4. Follow up. Specifically and quickly. That day, while it's fresh. And after that, follow up once more.

5. You are there to talk to the audience, not the speakers.

6. Use social media and relevant hashtags to let others know you're there and join in conversations as they happen.

Be brave, take a breath, walk up to someone and say hello. And have your lines ready to help you make a graceful exit and move on.

Emma Niven: Achieving an ambition to land one more big role

Whilst her boys were growing up, Emma worked as an independent consultant, a role that meant she was based from home and gave her the flexibility she needed. As the boys approached their late teens, she decided she was ready for a full time, permanent, employed position. One that would stretch and challenge her.

"I want to be on the 6.24 from Reading to London every day. I don't need flexibility. I've done my years of putting my career second while I raise my kids. They're both over 16 now. It's my turn. I reckon I have another big job in me. That's what I want."

After a search that took over two years that's exactly what she has. A senior role at a prestigious London law firm, running a number of strategic change projects. It required determination and persistence on her part, an enlightened recruiter, Totum Partners, and an employer that was willing to think laterally about what she could add to their team.

So how did Emma land the role?

"Talking to lots of people," she explains. "The first thing I needed to do, though, was figure out exactly what I could do. I had been a management consultant, I knew how partnerships worked and eventually I narrowed my focus to finding a change management type role for a law firm."

With a rough idea of the sort of opportunity she was looking for, Emma then set about meeting anyone who might be able to help: friends, their contacts, recruiters, acquaintances.

"All those meetings kept me in the market. It meant I had to get out of my jogging bottoms and look professional. And each time, I had to hone my story. I had to come across as someone serious and credible. And someone who was looking for work."

One recruiter was very specific, instructing Emma to "get yourself a sharp suit". She was frank, telling her that getting a senior role was going to be tough. She had been out of corporate life for a long time, she'd have to work very hard to be convincing. It was critical that she didn't look like "a mum who is balancing work and home" and she advised her to "use less domestic language".

Recruiters struggled with her lack of very recent employed experience. Eventually, she met Totum, who took a different view. They took time to understand Emma's skill set and thought about the clients they had who were looking to fill roles that needed them.

This approach was pivotal. Emma was introduced to Travers Smith, a city law firm, and was able to use the language of competencies to prove that she would be capable of all aspects of the role they were looking to fill. This in turn gave the HR Director recruiting her the ammunition she would need internally to explain why Emma had been hired into the role.

Emma couldn't be happier with what she's doing today.

"It's an odd shaped role, but that's fine – I've got an odd shaped CV. My title is Head of Projects, but it's a new role and doesn't sit in a large department, which is unusual. I don't have a natural peer group in the firm and no-one really understands where I sit in the hierarchy. I'm comfortable with that. I'm mature enough to have built my own networks and relationships in the firm and that's what I need to get the job done."

Her advice?

"Be persistent. Looking back, all those meetings were useful. Every one. You have to put on the uniform, you have to get your story straight. Go motivated and interested. Most people who can help, will help."

Your Checklist for the Chapter

✓ Have you thought about your opening lines for any networking event?

✓ Do you have a list of relevant contacts within your current network?

✓ Have you thought about how you could help them?

✓ Have you told them what you're looking for?

✓ Have you identified groups that could help you grow your network?

✓ If one doesn't exist that matches your passions, skills and interests, have you thought about forming one?

✓ Do you know who is running/offering events and courses that could be of interest to you?

Other Resources

Never Eat Alone: and other secrets to success, one relationship at a time by Keith Ferrazzi
The bible of networking.

Networking Know-how: connecting for success by Zoe Cunningham
An antidote. Same subject, different style. Written by a woman, packed with practical advice and wisdom.

4.

The tools of the trade: CVs, LinkedIn, interviews

Whatever else has changed about the job market, some things remain a constant. You're probably going to need a CV – and a LinkedIn profile to match. You'll also need to succeed at interview.

There are countless books and online resources on these subjects, along with people offering free and paid-for boot camps, webinars and workshops to help. Our purpose in this chapter is not to replace these – we'll provide some useful links at the end. Instead, our aim is to give you enough information to get started.

At She's Back we've been fortunate enough to work with the wonderful team at *City CV.*, founded by former headhunter and Goldman Sachs and Merrill Lynch Recruiter, Victoria McLean. Victoria's advice and support has been invaluable in helping us shape this chapter.

The chapter is split into three sections:

A. CVs and Today's Recruitment Processes

B. LinkedIn

C. Interviews

A. CVS AND TODAY'S RECRUITMENT PROCESS

This section will:

- Explain how technology has changed the way recruitment works today
- Help you write a compelling, crisp CV
- Point to other tools and resources that will help

What you need to know about the recruitment process

Traditional recruitment channels are not designed to help you find a job. They are designed to find the CV that best fits a job description as quickly as possible. There is a big difference.

Let's start with CVs. CVs are the current lynchpin of the recruitment industry – worth around £28 billion to the UK economy.

Most recruiters today use something called an 'Applicant Tracking System', or ATS. This is the first filter in the process of whittling down job applicants to decide who to call back for interview. Applicant Tracking Systems are simply a way of scanning a CV and matching it with the relevant job description. They use key words to compare one with another, and any CV which doesn't have the right number of key words will be rejected.

Other reasons for rejection include the use of tables, which some ATS can't read, logos, images and any sort of formatting that can't be understood by the system.

If your CV makes it through the ATS, your next problem is the human. The first pair of eyes to scan it are likely to belong to a relatively junior individual, who is incentivised to place as many people as possible as quickly as possible. Faced with a mountain of CVs that have made it through the applicant tracking system, these humans are highly skilled at discarding any that look problematic. A career break is often seen as problematic so you need to be savvy about providing compelling CV that will grab that human's attention.

The first question a recruiter will be asking is "Does this person have recent experience of doing the job I'm being asked to fill?"

If you're returning from a break, you're unlikely to have had recent relevant experience. Not only that, if you're writing it chronologically from now to the start of your career, it's likely that the first half of your CV doesn't do a great job of showcasing the full extent of your capability and potential.

> "I read the first page of Ayesha's CV and all it told me was that she was a mum who'd had various part-time jobs and done a bit of volunteering. It was only when I turned over that I found out she had 10 years' experience in supply chain manager for two multinational companies."

Many people won't bother with page two if they are not hooked by the first paragraph of page one. Your CV is a

SALES document. The very first paragraph – your executive summary – has to stand out. It is your business case, setting out why a company or organisation should hire you.

Your CV needs and deserves a lot of time and attention. At City CV, Victoria's team of professional CV writers would expect to spend at least 1-2 days on writing a client's CV: you should expect to do at least the same. And you will need to tailor your core CV for every job application.

KEY WORDS AND USING THE RIGHT LANGUAGE

Before we go into the detail of how to structure your CV, a note about key words, because they are so important. Using the right key words will help you get through the ATS and will enable the human recruiter to tick off their checklist.

They will vary depending on the job in question but there are some principles that apply in all cases. They tend to be specific, technical, expertise-based, rather than softer, more subjective behavioural traits. The best place to look is the job description, if there is one.

For example, here are some key words from a job description for a supply chain manager for an FMCG organisation:

- Service Level Agreements | Procurement | Purchasing | Supply Chain | Logistics | Project Management | Distribution Centre | Warehouse Management | FMCG

Or a job as a talent manager for a managed services company:

- Human Resources | HR subject matter expert
- Employee Branding
- Executive Assessment
- L&D | Learning and Development
- Performance Management
- Building Diversity
- Recruitment
- Talent Dashboard | Talent Metrics

Or a business development manager for a media company:

- Media agency experience | global networks,
- Digital Communication Channels
- Campaign planning
- Media buying
- FMCG Global brands/clients
- Project management
- Sales | Customer Retention | Account Management | Business Development | Sales Force | Customer Relationship Management

70% of CVs are screened by ATS so align your headings, key skills and job titles to the most commonly used industry terms – the industry standard, So no Head of Happiness or Chief Innovator or Head of Fame, please. Despite them sounding stupendous fun.

Remember ATS is only the first step and hopefully at some point your CV will be read by a real person – so find the balance between making it searchable and readable.

LANGUAGE

Try to avoid filling your CV with words that are too passive. It's tricky but some words have become clichés that just don't carry any meaning.

Detail oriented

Highly motivated

Multi-tasker   **Team player**

Excellent communication skills

Independent   **Flexible**

Strong work ethic

If the job description specifically says that you need excellent communication skills then of course do include it but provide context and evidence.

What you might be tempted to say:
"Excellent communication skills."

What would be a better thing to say:
"Rolled out new branding strategy to 2000 employees; designed and implemented communications plan that covered 12 offices."

For every role use active, achievement-based verbs to start every sentence. Here's Deb's example for a recent project:

Deb planned and orchestrated the final weeks of a pitch for a new building and engineering consortium that included her clients, Tate Harmer architects. Deb **refined** the creative ideas and headed the process of **designing** and **structuring** the technical content for an international architecture competition. Deb's role helped this team **win** the £15 million contract to redevelop the creative teaching facilities and theatre at York St John University.

Useful verbs include: chaired, controlled, coordinated, executed, headed, operated, orchestrated, organized, oversaw, planned, produced, programmed.

Working alongside a list is always useful to get the creative juices flowing when updating your CV. Google more. Have fun. Most of all try to avoid ubiquitous words such as responsible for, managed or led. Be specific. Say what difference you made. And sell it.

GUIDELINES FOR WRITING YOUR CV

Many recruiters and executive search firms have examples and templates for creating CVs on their sites. Whatever template you choose, here are some broad guidelines to help get your CV through the ATS and past a pair of human eyes to that all-important interview.

1. **Length:** No more than two pages. No arguments here, no-one is going to read more than two pages. And making the font really tiny is not an option.

2. **Style:** Write it in the third person and avoid all pronouns.

Firstly, it avoids you using the word 'I' every other line and it's easier to boast about yourself when it reads as though someone else is saying it. Women are notoriously bad at boasting about themselves

3. **Personal details:** Name, contact details, phone, address, email address. Victoria has been amazed at the number of CVs that don't have details of how to contact the candidate. Do NOT include your date of birth or a photo or your marital status. They are not relevant to modern CVs. Include a hyperlink (rather than a long list of words and numbers) to your website if you have one – and LinkedIn profile. Make it easy for the person reading your CV to click through to the information that will enhance your application.

4. **Executive Summary/Personal Statement:** The executive profile should be a concise, memorable synopsis of you, summarising why you should be hired. It's the equivalent of your elevator pitch and will need to be tailored for each job for which you apply.

   Some people will only continue to read your whole CV if that introduction is sufficiently compelling. It will take time to write, needs to include the right key words, and should sum up your business case. Who you are, what you're offering and what you're looking for.

   Unless it's wildly inaccurate, think about giving yourself the title of the job you're applying for. Here are a couple of examples of the first part of two different executive summaries:

EXPERIENCED CHIEF OPERATING OFFICER

Visionary COO with over twelve years' experience of delivering operational improvement projects to clients in sectors ranging from Financial Services to FMCG. Projects covered all back-office functions including HR, Finance and Technology.

FINANCIAL RISK AND CRIME LEAD

Senior risk, financial crime and regulation leader. A qualified barrister with eight years in crime and regulatory practice and more than a decade of experience defining and building regulatory and risk functions in the insurance industry.

5. **Key Skills:** Beneath the executive summary and before you describe your detailed work experience, provide a summary of the key skills you're bringing to the table.

    The question is, which ones and how many? In terms of how many, obviously it's a judgement call, but if you're listing more than 25 then it's hard to claim they are all 'key' skills. Look at the job description or, if one doesn't exist, think about the role you're going to apply for. What sort of skills will the person recruiting be looking for. Be specific and don't waste space with skills that are too basic or generic.

    To save space it's fine to list these key skills in bullet point form, perhaps in three parallel lists. On a very practical note, **do not put these in a table**. **An ATS cannot read tables**. It's fine to do three columns of bullet points but tables are a no-no.

"This section should include key words, specific to you, your function, your sector and your expertise. Ensure that anything you refer to here is backed up with tangible evidence in your professional experience, otherwise they are just bland platitudes – meaningless words with no real substance.**"**

Victoria McLean

6. **Work Experience:** This section is about providing sufficient evidence that you can do the job. Do not simply list your responsibilities. It's boring and being ***responsible*** for something doesn't necessarily mean you made anything happen.

List your work experience chronologically but be aware of the need to showcase the experience that's most relevant to the job you're applying for. There is no need to detail every role you've had during your career break unless it's relevant.

Bring your experience to life. Make it interesting. For each role, tell the story of what you were hired to do and how you added value. Focus on achievements and outcomes. Include as many facts and figures as possible. These could include, for example:

- Scale of a project you ran, budget and results.
- Impact on profits or revenues.

- Growth in customers or client base.
- Improvements to customer satisfaction.
- Efficiencies within the supply chain or process for which you were responsible.
- External recognition or awards.
- Employee satisfaction in your team.
- Career development of others.
- Innovations or new ideas that you introduced and the impact they had.

You'll also need to include details of your education, qualifications, language skills and any other information that's relevant to the role. Adding a section on 'hobbies and interests' makes it a bit more personal and gives you character but do take a little care with this. Apparently 'socialising with friends' is a pet hate for a third of recruiters.

HOW TO DEAL WITH THE CAREER BREAK

Rule number 1: Don't make a big deal out of it.

It's fine to simply put dates and Planned Career Break to explain why there's a gap in your work experience.

Rule number 2: If you're going to talk about what you did, make sure it's relevant.

Remember this is a sales document. Its job is to get you an interview. When you reach interview stage you'll undoubtedly be asked about what you did during your break but that doesn't mean it has to take up space here, unless it's relevant.

If you've retrained, taken on a voluntary role, become a trustee of a charity, completed a significant sporting achievement, become a governor, run a club and you think your experience is interesting and relevant, do mention it.

If you did several part-time roles, or lots of project work, rather than listing each one individually, group them together, with a focus on common themes, client satisfaction and deliverables.

Rule number 3: Avoid language that's too mumsy.

It puts people off.

Checklist for your CV:

Have you	Yes/No
Included up-to-date contact details	
Checked, double checked and checked again for spelling mistakes	
Had someone else review for spelling mistakes	
Included a summary that is a compelling case for why you could do the job	
Matched the key words in your key skills and experience to the key skills being asked for in the job description	
Kept it to 2 pages	
Dealt with any career gaps	
Ensured your work experience illustrates your achievements and outcomes	
Checked presentation – same font, easy to read, plenty of white space	
Included any **relevant** experience or skills gained during your career break	

COVERING LETTERS: WHAT AND WHY

The CV is all about presenting your qualifications and capability to do the job. The covering letter is about your MOTIVATION for doing that job.

Do not repeat all the information in your CV.

"Use your letter to show the pull factors, that you will be satisfied and fulfilled. If there is one thing that can clinch the deal (above all else), it's passion – employers hire individuals that love their job so don't be afraid of showing your motivations, excitement and enthusiasm." Victoria McLean

Open with an introduction explaining the job you're applying for and attaching your CV. There then needs to be three paragraphs in the body:

1. Why you are the perfect candidate for the job. A summary of the unique skills and experience you're offering.

2. Why you're excited about working for the company. Demonstrate that you understand where this role fits with their direction, look at how the job is advertised and reflect that back.

3. How you are particularly enthusiastic about this particular role and how you see yourself delivering value.

Here's an example from a covering letter that City CV helped to craft for one of their clients:

"I am particularly excited about the client management element of this role. At ABC, this was my key focus; I doubled budget in terms of client revenues and expanded wallet share with existing customers by 30%. I always find that when I love what I do I excel and find the client exposure in this post particularly attractive."

B. LINKEDIN

In this section we will:

- Outline the critical role of LinkedIn in today's recruitment market.
- Help you create a stand out LinkedIn profile.
- Explain how to use LinkedIn as part of your proactive search for a job.

Our original research reached over 1,300 women in an online survey and was backed up by face-to-face workshops for over 100. During those face-to-face sessions we talked to women about social media. What did they use? Facebook and Instagram were the most popular. Few used LinkedIn. And yet many of these women wanted to return to work. Where are all the jobs? LinkedIn.

We asked a few women why they were so averse to this platform. The results were illuminating.

Ayesha, for example, was looking to return after a six-year career break. As well as significant experience working in industry, consulting and banking she has an MBA from INSEAD. Over the course of her 15-year career she had gathered an impressive array of contacts. LinkedIn is an ideal way of reconnecting with people you used to work with, who can so often be key to helping you get an introduction. We asked her whether this was a route she was using. No. Why not?

"I don't use LinkedIn. I wouldn't know what to say about my career break. I'm embarrassed that all those people I used to work with have gone on to have great careers and I've just been a stay at home mum."

Forget the fact that she hasn't 'just' been a stay at home mum (the story is much more complicated than that), her reluctance to use what is probably **the** most important social media channel for job hunters was seriously damaging her efforts to return. As we pointed out in the chapter on networking, people generally love to help if you ask them. Reconnecting on LinkedIn is a way of saying hello and asking for that help.

CREATING A STAND OUT LINKEDIN PROFILE

LinkedIn is a critical part of the recruitment industry. It is used by recruitment companies to find candidates for jobs; it's a first port of call for many employers to check you out; it is an online reference checked by the people considering hiring you as part of their final due diligence; and it's where many of your old work colleagues hang out. If you're looking for work, you need to be on there.

Much of the advice is similar to that in the CV section above. Key words are just as important here. One key difference is that whilst you can have several CVs, all tailored for different job applications, you can only have one LinkedIn profile at a time. The other, is that whereas you need to keep a CV to two pages, there is much more opportunity on LinkedIn to go into detail about your skills and experience and also to gather recommendations from others.

There are also some other important nuances to LinkedIn that are important to know and useful for you as a returner. Over and above the advice on CVs, City CV would recommend:

1. Use a professional photo.

It's not OK to have a holiday snap. Or a landscape. You will end up going to meetings where the person you are meeting probably uses LinkedIn to remind themselves what you look like. Use a smart professional photo. And it's fine to smile; profiles with a smiley headshot get 25% more views.

2. Create a compelling summary.

> "Please don't copy and paste the summary section from your CV. This is an amazing opportunity to pitch yourself to a broad target audience. You have 2000 characters here to sell yourself. Use all of them!"
>
> Victoria McLean

There are many ways to do this. The important point is that a reader should come away with a clear idea of who you are and how you add value to organisations.

Be creative here, tell the story of your career to date, your successes and give some personality away. You could feature your core competencies, focusing on a number of key skills that you offer and what you intend to do in the future.

If appropriate, it's fine to end with a call to action, saying you are open to discussions about opportunities for A, B, C.

3. Detail your experience, being sure to use the key words relevant for your target positions.

This section should reflect the same sections on your CV. For SEO purposes, it is even more crucial here to use the right keywords. LinkedIn also provides you with the opportunity to add more detail on some of the projects you've been involved in, awards you've received and languages spoken in the Accomplishments section. Where CVs are limited to words, LinkedIn allows you to add links to videos and other media.

4. Connect with people.

Inevitably, on day one, you will have no contacts. It's up to you to create them. Go through your contacts and connect with relevant people. Use the search function to find old colleagues or work acquaintances. Yes, some will ignore you but so what. Most won't.

And here's a tip: when you search someone and look at their profile, check out what they are listing as their skills. If you've worked with someone and genuinely think they have that skill, endorse them for it (this is very straightforward when you're on the site). You never know, they may just endorse you back. At a minimum, you should be looking for 50 connections.

Say hello when you ask them to connect and either then or later ask for them to endorse you. It might feel a bit odd to begin with but it's common practice. You won't look strange.

5. Endorsements and recommendations

The endorsements section allows you to select key skills, for which people you have worked with can then endorse you. Aim to build up endorsements over time. The best way to have people endorse you? Endorse them first.

Recommendations are even more powerful but can easily fall through the cracks as you need to be proactive about asking for them and then tracking the results. They add a lot to your credibility on the site as someone has to actually take the time to write something, rather than just ticking a box for an endorsement.

Recommendations can come from former colleagues, bosses, mentors, clients, suppliers and anyone who has collaborated with you in some way. Have a strategy. Ask people and be clear with them what you're looking for. It's fine to suggest a potential recommendation and of course be proactive in recommending them back.

6. Follow people

Find people on LinkedIn whose work you admire or who you're interested in and follow them. You could choose key influencers – Arianna Huffington, Sheryl Sandberg and the like. Equally you could choose people who are working in your field who write articles and share pieces that are of interest.

Not only is this a great way of getting abreast of what's going on in your field, it's also going to be a valuable skill when it comes to you being your own recruiter (the chapter after this.)

7. Join Groups

Join some groups. There are thousands. Some are people with common interests – Social Media Marketing, for example – others could be alumni groups for certain organisations. Others are specifically created for people who have a similar skill set such as HR Grapevine or Strategy Consulting Network for instance.

The requirements could change but LinkedIn itself will tell you how far your profile is 'complete'. Currently, to have a 100% complete profile you need:

- A profile photo.
- 2 or more positions held, along with descriptions of your roles.
- 5 or more skills on your profile.
- A summary statement.
- Details of your industry and postal code.
- Where you went to school.
- 50 or more connections.

CREATING AHOW TO USE LINKEDIN TO FIND A JOB

Once you have a stand out LinkedIn profile, the next step is to be savvy and tenacious about using the platform to help you find work.

Assuming you have used the right key words, written a compelling summary, described the full extent of your experience and set out a little about your aspirations, you should be relatively easy to find by a recruiter doing a search for someone with your skill set.

Here are some other tactics you can deploy to help with your job search.

1. Let recruiters know you're open.

Under the dashboard section of your profile there is a button that can be used to tell recruiters you are open to new opportunities. Complete some basic information about the role you're looking for, location, industry and how actively you're looking, and you will be directed to current opportunities. Future searchers will pick up on your data.

2. Follow the companies and the people you are interested in working with.

By doing so you will receive updates when people leave, news about the organisation and most importantly open jobs that have been posted to the site. The company pages will also help you work out if you know anyone there who could potentially make an introduction.

3. Use the job search function

The jobs tab allows you to search for specific jobs, either simply through a title and location, within a specific sector or even at a particular company.

The results will show jobs that meet your specified criteria alongside other similar jobs that may be of interest. Have a look at the job descriptions and they will give an insight into the keywords that need to be included in your profile for you to come up in a search for that role.

We know that personal introductions are critical and searching on LinkedIn can also help here. Go back to your profile page and search for the same job title at a specific organisation and the results will throw out a list of people with the same or similar job title both there and elsewhere. It will also show where you have connections, enabling you to send a message or contact your connection for an introduction or further information.
Over time LinkedIn's intelligent search will get a feel for what your preferences are and give them to you.

4. Build up your recommendations.

As mentioned above, recommendations add more weight than endorsements. In effect, they are like mini-references. Think carefully about who could recommend you and have a plan to gather their comments for your profile.

5. Be proactive about using Groups.

Savvy recruiters create career groups to give them access to the best candidates, so join groups that match your career choice and region. Engage with conversations and debate in the groups you have chosen, which presumably connect to your career aspirations. Provide useful feedback and links to relevant articles; ask simple questions that can engage others; share research that others might find useful.

6. Continue to build your network.

Use thoughtful, tailored, short and well-written messages to continue to build your network. If you've met someone at a conference and have their business card, connect with them but make that request to connect personal.

7. It's not just about a Job.

There are currently over 500 million people on LinkedIn. It will only go up. This is currently *the* social media platform where employers and employees connect. Think of this not as a job site but as a place where you can build your connected future.

Checklist for your LinkedIn profile:

Have you	Yes/No
Included a professional photograph	
Created a summary profile that puts you at your best	
Included links to projects, videos and any other media where relevant	
Outlined all previous roles and employers	
Made connections with all relevant work colleagues and acquaintances	
Joined interesting and relevant groups	
Gathered recommendations and endorsements	
Checked how far your profile is from being 100% complete	
Let employers know you're open for business	
Identified who to follow in order to progress your career ambitions	

C. INTERVIEWS

In the chapter 'Being in the Room' we will discuss how to make an impact with presence and confidence. These skills are fundamental to performing well at interview.

Initial interviews could take place over the phone or on Skype. Whatever the medium being used, there are some fundamentals that you need to be aware of.

Here are our 10 commandments

1. It's a conversation: Think 50/50.

The very term interview makes people default into thinking that this is all about some guy behind a desk asking questions whilst you try to come up with plausible answers. Wrong. Well, partly wrong anyway.

A huge part of the impact you make has to do with how you make the interviewer feel. Not just about you but about themselves. Let them do some of the talking. Hear what they have to say. Not only will this lead to a more comfortable conversation, it will also give you the opportunity to listen to what they feel is important so that you can adjust your answers later on.

2. Research the company, the role and the individual.

You need to appear interested and enthusiastic, which is a little difficult if you haven't done your homework on the company and also on the role they are looking to fill. What's sometimes less obvious is the need to do a bit of homework on the person doing the interviewing.

If it's a first interview this can be tricky but if you're onto a second interview, the headhunter, recruiter or person who saw you first should be able to give you some guidance. What is this person like? What are they passionate about? What's their style?

Knowing all of this helps you think about how to develop some empathy and connection with that person during the interview.

Shaila had a second interview coming up with the CEO of a business services organisation. She was applying for a newly created role, the focus of which was to help them reposition their brand. Her first interview with the COO had gone well, and she had been able to use her prior experience to establish her credentials. She had also spent some time thinking about what the new brand position should be and how it could be created.

Prior to the CEO interview, she sought some guidance on his personality and what he might be looking for. The COO, who already knew Shaila could do the job, had this advice:

"Let him talk. He's passionate about where we need to take the brand and has his own ideas. He's also a father and will be keen to talk about that. He makes a point of leaving early one day a week, so he will totally get your need for flexibility."

This guidance meant that Shaila approached the interview very differently. She got the job, and on terms which suited her perfectly.

3. Prepare your opening lines.

"Tell me a little bit about yourself," is a very common way of opening an interview. It might seem like an innocuous question but it's perhaps the most important one you will be asked. It's your opportunity to present yourself, tell your story, and make that all important first impression.

Prepare and practice. Make sure your answer conveys your motivation to do the job and the experience you're bringing to bear. It should be no more than 60-90 seconds long.

4. What's behind the question

In most cases, the interviewer will have a checklist of things they have to tick off. Their questions are simply a way of going through that list. Essentially, they want to know if you're going to be able to do the job.

Some questions will focus on asking you about your competentcies – whether you have the skills required. Think about what those skills are (they will be there on the job description) and how your answers will help the interviewer tick the relevant boxes.

In many organisations, competency frameworks are used to describe what skills are required at different levels. Here's an extract from the competency framework of the OECD:

Competency area	Client Focus	Analytical thinking
Level 1	• Responds to and anticipates client needs in a timely, professional manner • Strives to meet service standards	• Gathers information from a variety of sources • Distinguishes between critical and irrelevant pieces of information
Level 3	• Anticipates clients upcoming needs and demands • Looks to add value beyond clients' immediate requests and acts on them	• Independently engages in tasks which require interpretation of complex sets of information • Identifies gaps in information and makes assumptions in order to continue analysis
Level 5	• Builds clients confidence using own personal reputation and expertise • Determines strategic direction and long-term opportunities to best meet clients' needs	• Is sought out by others for advice and solutions on how to interpret information • Discerns the level of pressure or emphasis to apply in each aspect of the analysis

If you were applying for a job here, at level 5, you would want to make sure you didn't simply talk about how you look to add value to clients, you would need to explain how, in previous roles, you were able to use your own personal expertise and reputation to make a difference.

Similarly, if you're asked to provide an example of, say, working in a team, the interviewer is probably hoping to tick off a few things: team playing; handling disagreement; empathy; communication; leadership.

Victoria's advice:

"It's so easy to get lost in the story in an interview. Candidates often make the mistake of retelling their story in great detail, without making sure they tick off all the things the interviewer is looking for."

5. Learn to stop.

20 seconds to 2 minutes is all it should take to answer a question. After that, it's time for a pause. If the interviewer needs to know more they'll ask. Go on much longer than 2 minutes and the likelihood is they will have lost the thread of what you're talking about.

"Give the interviewer time to catch up. They'll need to make notes. Go on too long and they're likely to drift off and start thinking about what's for dinner."

6. Whatever the question, have your answers.

However the questions are phrased, any employer really only wants to get the answers to 5 questions:

- Why do you want this job, really?
- What can you do for us? Can you help me?
- Are you our sort of person?
- What makes you different from the 89 other people I could interview for this job?
- Can we agree terms that suit us both?

7. Whatever the answers, have your questions.

This is a dating game. You need to have answers to questions of your own. You will inevitably be asked "What questions do you have for me?" Prepare some beforehand. They could be about:

- The industry or sector, what's happening today, future trends.
- This particular organisation, their positioning and strategy.
- The specific job you're applying for.
- The person doing the interview.

Whatever you do, don't ignore the last category of question. People love to talk about themselves and it will help you connect with the interviewer.

8. Manage the risk.

In any interview, there will be elements where your CV and experience does not quite fit what the company is looking for. Where you are effectively at a disadvantage. This represents a risk to the interviewer. Help them manage that risk.

Think about where your CV might be lacking in the appropriate experience well before the interview and find ways to address any concerns. For example, they might be looking for experience of negotiation which you didn't do in your previous job. However, you might have had plenty of experience of negotiation in some of the activities you've undertaken during your break. Identify any gaps and work out how to close them. Be on the front foot.

9. Make your answers clear and succinct.

Like this point.

10. Interview with confidence.

Presenting a confident persona not only makes you come across as credible, it also puts the interviewer at ease. Chapter 6, Being in the Room, is full of advice and exercises to help you practice this.

WHAT TO SAY ABOUT THAT CAREER BREAK

"We imagine that when we are thrown out of our usual ruts, all is lost. But it is only then that what is new and good begins. While there is life there is happiness. There is much, much before us."

Career breaks are a little bit like the war. "Don't mention it." Professional guidance from recruiters advise us to skip over the break. We think this is profoundly misguided. To skip over a career break is to collude with the myth that nothing useful happens outside of work. That could not be further from the truth. In an age where, assuming we start work at, say 21 or 22, we all face a working life of upwards of 40 years, so who isn't going to need a break at some point? It could be because of children, to go travelling, to look after elderly relatives or simply to recharge your batteries. It will happen to more and more of us.

Take the lead. Change the conversation. Signpost the new, shinier improved you without apology or qualification.

So what do you say?

1. **I'm refreshed, re-energised and re-focused.** Who isn't better after a break? And when you decide to return, putting in place the childcare and support to make it work, any new employer can be sure you are 100% committed. With something to prove and fire in your belly to prove it.

2. **I am so much more productive**. Minus a salary and the suffocating bureaucracy inherent in most large organisations, we tend to become slicker, speedier. Less time to faff. If you've been juggling other people's needs with your own, carrying four timetables in your head, you are more efficient. Guaranteed.

3. **I've broadened my skills, knowledge and experience.** Smash the myth that you turned off that busy brain. You still read, absorbed, thought and contributed. You knew what was happening in the world and in the world of work. You didn't check out. Be specific about what skills you have now, give examples of how you developed them. Add what do you know now that you didn't know before?

4. **I've grown and deepened my network.** I have more references and a wider range of organisations, people and situations to call upon, ask, tell things to or reference. Institutions can make us myopic. You've seen more than what is in these four walls.

5. **I've witnessed – and can share – different ways of getting things done**. Things we can learn from. That's healthy. Leadership styles and ways of delivering are all around us – schools, hospitals, retail, travel. You've embraced other forms of comms, identified what works – and what doesn't.

6. **I have new perspectives on customers and clients.** You have more insight because you've been out there more, interacting with the world as a consumer or creator or been on the receiving end of services. You know how it feels and how it could be improved. You have acquired those elusive empathy skills, by osmosis.

7. **You can trust me.** I have delivered without the comfort blanket of a large organisation. I've dealt with my own IT, worked out the fastest ISP, I've navigated the complexities of new technology tools or systems. I've learned independently. I've set my own milestones and frameworks for projects or travel or to help other people.

And finally – dare we say it – you are older. With less time to waste. Life is speeding up, as are you.

Back these up with examples. What was 'new and good' in your break? Help an employer understand. Be brief. Be brave. Know your own value. And negotiate the hell out of your return.

Other Resources

Tools for job seekers

If you're struggling or need a checklist or boost, there are resources that help you compare your CV against keywords. Examples include:

Job Scan – a fantastic resource for job seekers. You can upload both a job description and your CV. The site has a tool which will match the two and tell you how well your CV meets the requirements of the job.

Wordle.net – a tool that's great fun to use – it generates 'word clouds' from text that you provide. Simply copy and paste the job description and it will create a cloud of keywords.

Hunter.io – If you're trying to get in touch with someone but don't have their email address this website helps you find it.

Books

What Color is Your Parachute? 2018: A Practical Manual for Job-Hunters and Career-Changers by Richard Bolles

The CV Book: How to avoid the most common mistakes and write a winning CV by James Innes

The 2-Hour Job Search: Using Technology to Get the Right Job Faster by Steve Dalton

Steal the Show, from speeches to job interviews to deal closing pitches by Michael Port

5.

Being in the room

Actors call it being in the moment. Some leaders are described as possessing charisma. Others talk about having the elusive quality of presence. All well and good but what does this mean and why is it so critical? It's critical because when you're trying to make new connections, or finding a job, you're selling yourself. You have to make an impact. And this will depend not just on what you say but **_how_** you say it.

> **"**I've learned that people will forget what you said, people will forget what you did, but people will never forget how you made them feel.**"**
> Maya Angelou

Deb's deep experience in theatre provides the frameworks and references here. She's had years of using this expertise to help her clients win competitive pitches, deliver at conferences and lead presentations with impact and confidence.

What this chapter will do is take some of those lessons and help you sell yourself – in interviews, when networking and when meeting new people. We are going to work with your story, improvise and explore what techniques work to get you in the room.

What's different about this chapter is you need a partner for the exercises – a trusted friend. This is experiential learning, learning by doing. You have to do these exercises (they make little sense on paper), hear what you sound like, and see what you look like saying it. It's virtually impossible to do this alone and be objective.

Have an open mind. Roll with these exercises. These are some of the key delivery skills that help land a clear message immediately. And if you start strong you will be imbued with confidence for the rest of the conversation.

> **"**In the first thirty seconds, grab 'me by the throat and don't let go.**"**
> Billy Wilder, Film Director

Find your partner. Call yourselves Partner A (**A**) and Partner B (**B**) You are A, B will watch, listen, direct and feedback. It may all be giggly at first. Persevere – it's worth it.

1. Create some content.

For these exercises to work, you will need to have a few scripts to explore and practise. These could include:

1. Your elevator pitch of approximately one minute.
2. How you're going to introduce yourself at a networking event – 20 – 30 sends max.

3. Answer to the questions: What have you been doing during your break or why do you want this job?

Write these down on separate pieces of paper. A few short sentences grammatically correct.

The words are your script.

TIP – write as you speak, in your own vernacular and idiom. If you don't say good morning don't write it on paper. It's about being completely authentic and making it flow with your references and words, delivered with skill.

> **Example:**
>
> Kay is an architect who was Head of Design at the London 2012 Olympics and is looking to return after a career break. Here's an example of her scripted responses to the question "What did you do in your career break?"
>
> *The first thing I did was sort out our home and finances. They were in chaos. We then took on a major house renovation, which I project managed when the contractors left. That was quite a challenge because there were multiple suppliers all with different views. It was my responsibility to bring them all together, to resolve conflicts and manage the budget. It became a full-time job.*
>
> *I also was keen to maintain my network in the architectural world. I didn't want anyone to think I had disappeared. Through my contacts I was asked to help with a number of projects including one with Cross Rail, which was fascinating. That helped me keep up to speed with what's going on in construction generally, and obviously it's one*

of the largest projects that we've ever undertaken as a country. So being part of that was great.

I'm now studying for an MSc part time in Infrastructure, Investment and Finance which I'll complete at the same time my youngest goes to University.

This should give you the flavour of the sort of length of script you will need to work with for this exercise.

Now take some time to write yours. Don't be shy.

EXERCISE

A Stand up. Read out your own script. Neutrally. Just the words – don't explain.

B Please listen, don't interrupt and question. Feedback clearly on content:

- Did it sound authentic – was it representative of the way **A** speaks?
- Did the words make sense, were they specific and accessible?

The words should sound like **A** is talking to a reasonably intelligent, interested friend.

- Was it concise and precise?

If not, help them edit. Now ask **A** to refine the content following your observations. Ask them to do it again. Tell them why it is better.

2. Moderate your pace.

EXERCISE

A Say your revised version of the words out loud.

B Ask her to repeat the whole speech but taking twice the amount of time. Use a timer here. You're encouraging A to slow down, significantly.

B Tell her the effect of slowing down. Has **As** voice lowered, does she appear more calm, more controlled, more authoritative? Ask, did it give her more time to consider what she was saying? Offer feedback of the two versions and ask her how she will remember to slow down.

Why? When we are nervous (because we care about the outcome of something) we tend to speed up. It's very important to consciously modify your speed to allow people enough time to absorb what you're saying. It's about what they hear, not what you say. We need to try to avoid babbling and saying too much.

Slowing down also projects an aura of being in control and one of calm. If you do sound in control slowly this will help you feel more control.

3. Project.

EXERCISE

B Move to the other side of the room – a decent distance away. Ask **A** to repeat the words but increasing the volume. Subtly. Ask her to imagine she's saying the words as if they were arrows, aiming to shoot through you rather than land at your feet. Yes, a strange image. Be a rigorous director – this requires energy and commitment from **A**.

B Note the change in **A**'s voice. Was there more energy, clarity and exactitude in her pronunciation? Was it easier to listen to?

B Watch out for **A** cadencing – dropping volume and tone at the end of sentences. It's normal in deferential speech but not that useful in professional situations.

A small amount of projection helps to signal a gear shift. You're not chatting to a friend in a cafe – it should have a similarly relaxed tone but it is a different context. More crucially, a projected voice is easier to listen to. It has a greater degree of variety in pitch and tone. Above all else we want to make it as easy as possible for people who are listening to us to stay listening, engaged and remember what we want them to remember.

Now switch to a different question response from the three examples suggested. A longer example if possible.

4. Breath.

Controlling your breath is the easiest way to remain in focus, calm and support a clear message. It's both simple and profound when done well. The next exercise is a technique used by actors to help navigate long speeches, monologues and soliloquies. It helps to break the speech up in a way which makes sense to the audience by forcing the actor to think: "What am I saying? Why am I saying it? How am I saying it?"

The punctuation is there to help you. In a number of ways. It can slow down your fight or flight response mode, it can buy you time to answer and collect examples, suggestions and experiences. It gives the listener time to absorb what it is you've just said.

Using this simple technique forces us to be very present, aware of what is happening right now, avoiding worrying. When we pause we can consider: what is the real question, how are they responding to me, do I need to say more or be quiet? It encourages us to be aware of the impact we are having on people at that moment as well as what we are projecting.

EXERCISE

B Please ask **A** to go back to the script and note all of the punctuation – full stops and commas. Ask her to read it again, slowly and with projection of course, but thinking about breaking it up. Every time there is a form of punctuation direct them to:

- Stop.
- Be Silent.
- Breathe **out** – momentarily. Note, not breathe in. Breathing in is instinctive. We want to release not increase tension at this point.
- Only begin to speak when she is ready – aiming her words forward, projected and speaking slowly.

She will probably require lots of encouragement, as it may feel and appear very mechanical and awkward initially.

B Ask **A** to walk when they speak and be still when they are taking a moment to breathe out. Note and feedback on the two states. **A** should now be energised, purposeful and clear when talking OR silent and still using the out breath. The silences are active – they are times to gather her thoughts, regain control and prepare.

B Ask if it helped give her more control and thinking time? Did her voice appear stronger? Remind her how powerful silence is.

5. Expression and eye contact

EXERCISE

B Ask **A** to read once more either standing or seated. Note their facial expression and where they look

Does **A** appear enthusiastic, open, informed or curious? Or is **A** presenting a neutral, quasi-professional face, one that's hard to read and respond to? Do they make eye contact with you? Tell them – no one else will. Please remind them that an expressive face is more compelling than a passive one.

B Be honest. Please tell **A** what messages you're receiving through her facial expressions alone. What's the story? Remind her that words are 20% of our message. Encourage **A** to not be frightened to show how she feels. If she's happy to meet someone, show it.

Offer **A** direction on her eye contact. The gaze shouldn't be held for too long that it feels uncomfortable. Or marginally creepy. Watch out for **A** looking up when she is thinking. Note this and let **A** know if she does this habitually.

B Does **A** smile at any point? What effect does this have on you watching? When someone smiles it alters the voice. Try closing your eyes and listening again with **A** smiling – does **A**'s voice change when she smiles?

At She's Back we make a point of shaking hands, firmly, holding eye contact, introducing ourselves and starting a dialogue with how pleased we are to be there. We always, always smile; it's universal, free and it works. Old fashioned business courtesy that remains timeless in value.

6. Be congruent with your message.

Exercise

A You're speaking with control, delivering the words with energy and expression, looking your audience in the eye when you need to. Wonderful. Well done. Read again, please.

B Please watch but cover your ears.

What signals is she communicating with her body? Is **A** communicating the same message you've just heard non-verbally? Is it aligned and congruent? Look at her from the neck down, is her message connecting throughout?

B Direct **A** to practice these to help:

- Ask **A** to centre her feet, placing them hip distance apart and balance her weight evenly. Look for a sense of being strong and centred. This signals assurance and clarity. Is she loose and relaxed so the position isn't stilted or forced?

- Either sitting or standing – encourage **A** to lengthen her spine, lift her sternum and feel the crown of her head lifting towards the ceiling. What does this look like? This will radiate confidence and a strong sense of self. Remind her that she has years under her belt and heaps of social and intellectual capital. Help her reflect that through her body, with ease.

- Finally, does **A** use gestures with control and ease? Are they serving a purpose – are they adding to the message? Or is the piece of paper or screen or pen she is holding blocking communication?

A Think about two or three of these techniques that were effective. Ask **B** what techniques made the biggest difference. Don't try to do everything all at once. Focus on two or three things, practice until they become a habit. Rehearse this until those techniques become easy, fluid and compelling. You at your best.

An obvious point to note is that you won't have a script in discussion. Hopefully these exercises will help you memorise and prepare with structure and rigour.

Final exercises

A Practise without the script and think about what phrases have stuck and feel natural. What have you missed off from your original document? The important content should now have floated to the surface and be memorable.

And can you articulate with the same degree of expression, freedom and energy while sitting down? It is more likely you will be seated at an interview or meeting. The same principles apply so try one more time with **B** watching and note what changed when you didn't have the same freedom as you did when on your feet, moving around.

The secret... Think of all of these tips as secret weapons. Something extraordinary happens when we stop worrying about ourselves. We relax. Turning our attention to simple techniques directs our focus away from worrying about what others think of us. By concentrating on the exercises, we free ourselves up and speak more fluidly and naturally.

We are trying to avoid thinking about what has happened or what could happen and silence our inner critic. Be present, alert and engaged.

The point of these exercises is to set yourself up to tell your story with confidence. We know both from our research and experience that a lack of confidence can be a barrier to many women returning or stepping up.

You might think you are alone in lacking in confidence when it comes to presenting or interviewing. The fact is all actors worth their salt and most senior people have to work at this. It's a skill we can all develop. They like you, suffer from nerves – huge stage fright in many cases.

The Olivier award winning actress Juliet Stevenson CBE has spoken very movingly about how stage fright and debilitating nerves halted her career in her mid-forties.

> **"**I only had stage fright once, but it was quite a sustained period, for about two to three years. It was really frightening because it's like a disease, once it gets into your brain it's like something in your bloodstream.**"**
> Juliet Stevenson

She was terrified that she would never have the confidence to work again. Out of the blue she was offered a dream lead role in a Samuel Beckett play. Her method was to learn to deal with fear physically in the hope she would build up some psychological tools for dealing with her psychological fear. Juliet became a sporting daredevil – paragliding, skiing and even wing-walking. These exercises 'cured' her.

Yes, nerves can paralyse even the very best of us at any point. Leaders are coached, practise and rehearse. You can too. Having presence and making an impact is a skill we can all develop.

Your Checklist for this Chapter

✓ Have you thought about what you're saying about yourself in advance? Have you created your scripts?

✓ Can you deliver your script at a relaxed pace?

✓ Are you comfortable with how to project and use your breath?

✓ Have you practised saying it out loud?

✓ Have you done so with an audience and asked them to tell you what you look like?

✓ Does your story flow and feel like you when you don't have a piece of paper in front of you?

Other Resources

Presentation Zen: Simple Idea on Presentation Design and Delivery by Garr Reynolds
The go to for elegant, simple slides and excellent on structure.

Perfect Pitch: The Art of Selling Ideas and Winning New Business by Jon Steel
A very well written book full of stories including the winning pitch to host the 2012 Olympic Games in London.

Act Natural: How to Speak To Any Audience by Ken Howard
Combines content from his Harvard Lectures and as a successful actor in a very helpful guide.

Presence: How to use Positive Energy for Success in Every Situation by Patsy Rodenburg
Ex Head of Voice at The National Theatre. All of her books are excellent on vocal techniques we can all practice and get better at.

6.

Back to business

You are clear in your head that it's time to reignite your career. You have a compelling story about what you want to do and why you're a valuable asset. You're brimming with confidence, your CV rocks and your LinkedIn profile shows just how well networked you are.

Now all you need is a job.

Or do you?

Let's reframe that by talking about 'work' rather than 'a job'. Yes, sometimes people returning do want a permanent job. Emma, for instance, was clear that after years of independent project work, she wanted a full on, stretching, permanent job. Mel, on the other hand, having left a permanent, well paid, structured job to set up the Black British Business Awards, found that autonomy and variety were too important. She resolved to remain independent.

There are myriad of ways of finding work. What works best for you depends, in part, on your own personal aspirations and circumstances. In this chapter we will look at:

A. Back to Work: become your own recruiter. How to use the strategies, skills and tactics of an expert recruiter to land yourself a job.

B. **Who's Got Your Back:** specialist recruiters and programmes. People and places who connect you with work.

C. **Back With a Difference:** portfolio careers. Why they might be the right route for you.

This is not an exhaustive list. We do not, for instance, cover what it takes to start up and run your own business – an interesting option for more and more women. We have focused on these three as the most viable ways of finding well paid, meaningful work that utilises your previous experience and skills.

A. BACK TO WORK: BECOME YOUR OWN RECRUITER

Congratulations. You have a job. You are a top class recruiter. You have one client. Yourself.

We are very grateful to Stephanie Dillon, founder of *Inclusivity*, an agency which specialises in supporting people who are looking to reignite their careers. Stephanie has helped shaped the advice contained in this section, which is unashamedly 'How to get a job'.

We will:

- Outline the fundamentals of the labour market.
- Explain how to establish where you are going to be most competitive.

- Discuss how to pivot your career.
- Set out how to be proactive about finding a job.
- Describe the level of effort involved.

LABOUR MARKET FUNDAMENTALS

The labour market is a place where workers **compete** to secure the best jobs and employers **compete** to hire the best talent. It's a **competition.**

There. We've said it.

As a recruiter, you're in competition with others to find your candidate (you, remember) a job. You're going to need skill, tenacity and above all else the ability to **sell** your candidate. Selling is a key competency of a recruiter.

A fact: **flexible roles are not advertised very widely.** A 2017 survey by the flexible working experts Timewise found that less than one in 10 quality jobs – defined as those paying £20,000 FTE or above – are advertised as being open to flexible working options.

There are sites that specialise in flexible work, but you cannot simply rely on the recruitment market to surface flexible roles for you.

Most roles are advertised as being full time. Don't let that put you off.

In our research, almost a third of women who had returned found jobs that were originally advertised as full time for which they successfully negotiated flexibility. One way to negotiate part-time work is to strategically go for a job where they can't afford you and then negotiate a 4 or 3 day week for the same salary, so that your expertise becomes affordable.

Be realistic about what you're looking for. If you were previously full-time and want to go back three days a week on exactly 60% of your salary in a similar role, you may well find it a challenge. It's not impossible but could take time and effort to find and negotiate.

Be both ambitious and realistic in setting your goals and the parameters around your search. Understand the market you're in; and then prepare to compete in that market.

WHERE ARE YOU MOST COMPETITIVE?

You need to establish where you're most likely to win in this market. Competitive advantage usually comes from two broad areas:

1. The skills and competencies you have acquired to date.
2. Industry or sector knowledge.

Take Rashmi. She graduated in engineering and joined a multinational automotive manufacturer, where she was trained in Six Sigma and Total Quality Management process improvement techniques along-side core supply chain management skills. Prior to taking a career break, her 15-year career included a stint with a firm supplying parts to the automotive sector and a shift in geography and sector when she took on a supply chain management role with a pharmaceuticals company in Switzerland.

When considering returning, she could either choose to compete using her skills and competencies as a source of competitive advantage, or her knowledge of the automotive and pharmaceuticals sectors.

1.   A skills and competency lens

Where am I most competitive?

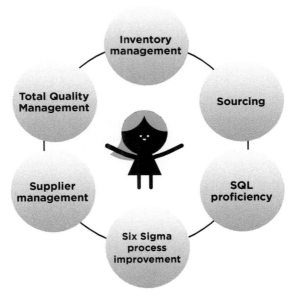

Skills & competency lens

This is an example and not intended to be exhaustive. Assuming she wasn't keen on returning to the Swiss pharma company, Rashmi could choose to use her core supply chain management skills – supplier management, sourcing, six sigma, SQL – to take on a similar role elsewhere, perhaps targeting roles in scale up ventures that needed to add professional skills in this area as they grow or potentially looking for opportunities as a consultant.

2. Industry or Sector Knowledge

Where am I most competitive?

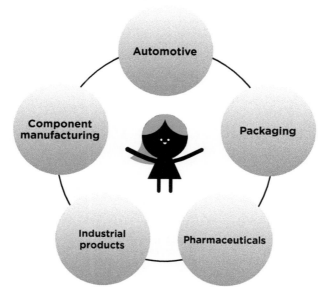

Industry/Sector lens

The other alternative is to take an industry or sector lens. Rashmi's experience was primarily of automotive, components, industrial products. During her 15-year career, she had lots of experience managing diverse teams. As an experienced, well qualified woman in a heavily male dominated sector, she could take her knowledge to look for new roles, perhaps related to talent acquisition and development, in these sectors.

If your job search is not leveraging one aspect of your competitive advantage, you are giving yourself a mountain to climb.

What would your own skills lens look like? Why not try on the following blank diagrams:

Where am I most competitive?

And what would your industry/sector lens look like?

Where am I most competitive?

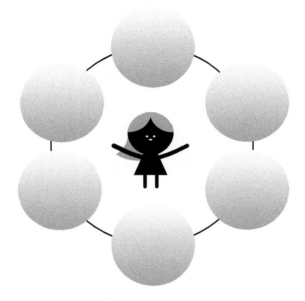

PIVOTING YOUR CAREER

Career breaks often make people think hard about their future working life. Half the women in our survey of returners went back to the same sector, often in a different role. We call this 'pivoting' your career.

How easy it is to pivot depends on what you're aiming for and how far it strays from your competitive advantage. It is plausible to think that Rashmi could target a role with a global distribution company, despite never having worked in that sector because she has deep supply chain experience.

Making a wholescale change is another issue. If Rashmi

decided that what she really wanted to do was take on a fundraising role for a charity, she would find it difficult. She has no experience of the charitable sector and no skills around fundraising. Making this change would require a number of steps. The first might be to take on a corporate social responsibility project or role for an automotive company where she understands the culture and operations.

Being able to pivot your role is, in part, about having the right level of confidence and understanding yourself. It is also, though, about being credible as a candidate in this new field.

How an Oil and Gas graduate used breaks to pivot her career through advertising to the charitable sector.

Zoe Warren, an HR specialist, has pivoted her career a number of times. She had significant health problems as a child and as an adult became deafened overnight, a disability she has not let hamper her career.

After completing the Exxonmobil graduate programme in HR, Zoe rapidly progressed to a regional HR lead role for the Royal Bank of Scotland. She found the political environment at the bank frustrating and unproductive and left to find something she felt was more real and meaningful.

She was able to land a job in what was then a relatively new tech and digital sector, joining a small, dynamic agency running their HR function. Zoe loved every moment, including helping to prepare the now highly respected agency for sale.

Whilst she loved the role, Zoe now had a young family and wanted to be able to spend time with them. She needed a similar role with a totally different working pattern.

Whilst on maternity leave, she was asked by a contact to help integrate a digital and direct marketing agency following its acquisition by a larger firm. This time it was a part-time consultant role, which combined perfectly with a young family.

Zoe's next career break was more complex. Her second maternity leave coincided with a period of ill health and she took time out to consider carefully where she wanted to focus her energy. This time, she wanted to use her HR expertise in the medical sector. Through Timewise, she found a part time role with a small start-up, working three days a week.

The flexibility was great, but Zoe missed the thrill of the creative sector. Having proved she could deliver on three days a week, she spotted an irresistible opportunity, again through Timewise, to work for Zone, an independent digital agency with a very large pro-social roster of clients. Zoe oversaw three mergers and saw Zone become Europe's biggest independent agency, ultimately helping them prepare for a sale to a Fortune 250 Company.

Zoe then took her only wholly voluntary career break, driven by the desire to support her daughter during exams.

She now has her own consulting business and spends time volunteering as an HR consultant for charities including Action on Hearing Loss.

> **"**I've had to take some time off for health reasons and I've still had a career so I guess that's the lesson for the book.**"**

BEING PROACTIVE ABOUT FINDING A JOB

Part of your job search will be reactive. Identify publications and newsletters where jobs are advertised – each sector usually has a first port of call for job ads. Do you know yours? As well as sector specific publications, there are more generic magazines, websites and job boards that advertise on a regular basis.

Identify platforms, sites, publications and newsletters that have a track record of advertising the types of jobs you're interested in. Include relevant Twitter handles as they will often communicate new opportunities.

However, reactive job searches can be tough. When you see a job advertised, it's probably been out there for a while and several other candidates will be looking and applying. That's not to mention any internal candidates that have perhaps already been approached about the role.

Your search is much more likely to be successful if you are proactive – which is exactly what a recruiter would be.

A proactive job search is a very systematic, logical process which requires commitment, some lateral thinking and a dogged determination. Qualities possessed by all the best recruiters.

You're at your desk. You know the sort of job you're looking for. What you now need to do is land some interviews. You need to build a target list and have a spreadsheet going that you can use as a tool to prompt action and check progress.

Here are the key steps to the process:

1. Explore who is hiring people with your skills set. Research specific companies if you have any in mind and look at recruiters who operate in your sector, jobs boards and LinkedIn.

2. Build a target list of organisations you think you'd like to work for.

3. Identify the key people who could be involved in hiring people into the sort of roles you are looking for.

4. Find out where they post jobs – as well as recruitment sites, jobs boards and direct recruitment, some also advertise on Twitter.

5. Go through your contacts to find out if you already know someone there who could help with an introduction.

6. If not, identify who, ideally, you'd like to connect with.

7. Build a plan – keep it manageable.

8. Set targets for yourself and be methodical.

Org'n	Website	Key people	Where they post jobs	Open jobs	My contact	Action	Next Steps

NB This is a **TOOL**. Its purpose is to help you land an interview. Filling in the form is not the end in itself. Adapt it as you see fit, it's there to help. And it's probably not wise to target more than 15- 20 organisations or the whole thing will become too laborious.

If you already have someone in your network who can make an introduction, and you've nailed your elevator pitch, you can hopefully begin to meet people to explore opportunities.

If not, all is not lost. Technology is your friend here.

1. Use LinkedIn.

LinkedIn in particular has removed many of the old barriers to making connections with new people, particularly the important ones who tend to make hiring decisions but who used to sit in large offices guarded by very fierce and protective personal assistants. No longer.

Work out who you'd like to connect with and follow them on LinkedIn. Track what they are interested in, read what they are posting and sharing. Like them. Comment, if appropriate, share onwards, provide them with something they might find interesting or useful. Your name will become familiar, enabling you to connect, which then means you can message them.

This may sound weird but trust us, it's not. Steph secured a fantastic project by following her own advice.

She knew Virgin Money were committed to diversity, so she found out who was responsible for HR and Recruitment and followed them on LinkedIn. One person shared an HR article in which he had written about Virgin's efforts around diversity. Steph liked the article and messaged Virgin Money's him to ask if he had thought about the returning talent market. He hadn't, but thought it sounded interesting and put Steph in touch with the someone in Newcastle who could well be interested. Steph made contact, took herself up to Newcastle and Virgin Money asked for her help in establishing their inaugural returnship programme.

All from a standing start. You can do this.

2. Use your own Network.

The point of Chapter 4, 'The Power of the Network', was not to create a whole load of new friends. The point of building your network is to increase the chances of you knowing someone who could make an introduction for you. Not necessarily to the hiring manager or the person responsible for recruitment but perhaps someone who works for the organisation you're targeting or knows someone else who is there.

Ask for an introduction. Make it easy by giving your contact the information they will need to do that introduction – your elevator pitch.

3. Consider referral programmes.

Many companies are trying to cut the fees they pay to recruiters and one way they do this is to offer bonuses to any employee who successfully makes an introduction to a successful future hire. If you know someone who's working at your target company, this gives them an added incentive to try to help you.

Conversely, look at your network and understand where they work – could they be the source of an interesting opportunity?

4. Don't be afraid to ask for help.

People are generally happy to be asked for helped. Clearly, don't just wing your CV over and ask for a job. Write to say you've noticed that they are winning awards for their innovation (or whatever), telling them that you're interested in the sector and love what their company is doing, asking if perhaps they would be kind enough to glance over your CV and give you some advice.

Asking for a favour is quite different from asking, directly, for a job. And it's a way of making one of those all-important connections.

5. Don't Give Up.

Remember, the point of this process is to make some connections, to open some doors and ultimately to get you to a position where you have an interview for a job. This will take some persistence. There is plenty of research into the sales process and evidence suggests that it takes seven contacts to get to a face-to-face appointment.

You can expect something similar.

Speaking again to Steph about her time in the recruitment industry, she relayed the story of having a new person start on her team.

"Realistically, for a new person starting with no book of contacts, I'd expect them to make their first placement within three months. And to do that they'd be looking at making 20 calls a week, doing 3 client visits a week and sending out 10-20 speculative CVs."

By speculative CVs she means contacting a hiring manager and sending them – with permission from the candidate – the CV of a candidate who they think should be considered for the job.

> **"**It's a job finding a job.**"**

How selling her story helped a Transformation Director land a new role.

Helen has a background in journalism and technology and has been involved in the transformation of the print media sector as it adapts to the constant demands of the digital revolution. She had reached a senior level and was looking for a new challenge. When she was headhunted for a similar role at a competitor it seemed an obvious move and she accepted the job.

Something was niggling at the back of Helen's mind, though. Would this really be a new challenge? She soon realised the answer to this was no, and decided to leave before it was too late, without the offer of a new role to go to.

Helen considered approaching recruiters but was reluctant. She knew from prior experience that they would be very keen on placing her in the same role in the same sector and not so keen on helping her pivot her career to a new sector or a different shaped role.

She became her own recruiter and quickly landed herself an interview that just as quickly turned into a job. How? She created a story about what she was looking for and she used her networks to get that story out there.

"I knew what my technical skills were," she told us "but that didn't feel like the whole story. So I asked people I'd worked with, what they would say about me."

Helen's original training was in journalism, so she wasn't entirely surprised when the answer came back:

"You ask really good questions. You seem to be able to explain the technology change in a way that people understand. You get why they're going to be worried about it and can then help explain what's in it for them."

So Helen's elevator pitch was something along the lines of:

"I've a 15-year track record of working in the media sector, running technology driven transformation programmes. My interests and expertise lie in helping people navigate what that means for them and the way they work. I'm looking to work with an organisation which is facing similar levels of disruption and needs to bring along large numbers of people for those changes to be successful."

Helen has always enjoyed connecting with other people and learning about new and emerging trends, regularly attending events run by organisations like 10 Digital Ladies, Mums in Tech and keeping in touch with ex-colleagues. It was through an old colleague that she made a connection at a large bank which is undertaking a huge transformation programme. That led to a meeting, which led to an interview, which led to a new job.

Bypassing the recruitment industry and with the same level of flexibility that she had in her previous role.

Your Checklist for this Section

✓ Are you prepared to compete?

✓ Have you pinpointed where you are most likely to win?

✓ Have you considered all the ways you could pivot one move?

✓ Have you a target list for the organisations you would like to work for?

✓ Do you know where jobs you're interested in are likely to be advertised?

✓ Do you know who is recruiting?

✓ Do you have a process for building your contact base and tracking your search?

✓ Are you systematic about your use of LinkedIn to surface job opportunities and connect with people who are hiring?

✓ Do you have a realistic view of how long this is likely to take? And have you set time aside?

B. WHO'S GOT YOUR BACK: SPECIALIST RECRUITERS & PROGRAMMES

More people are recognising the untapped potential of women who took a career break and are ready to return. Some organisations are doing something different to help women reclaim their careers. In this section we'll provide an overview of:

- Returnship programmes
- Specialist recruiters
- Tailored contracts
- Industry and sector initiatives

RETURNSHIP PROGRAMMES

The concept of an internship for mid-career professionals, coming back to work after an extended break, was first introduced by the late Brenda Barnes, then chief executive of the US food giant Sara Lee.

> **"**There's a large pool of women who chose to leave the workforce. But it doesn't mean they lost their brains.**"**
> Brenda Barnes

Many of today's returnship programmes follow a pattern she put in place at Sara Lee: returners are offered a short-term, paid contract (usually for 3-6 months), with a strong possibility of an ongoing role at the end of the programme. Most also offer additional support in the form of mentoring, training or coaching. They are primarily targeted at people who have taken a career break of more than 2 years and usually occur annually with a cohort of between 3 and 12 joining at the same time.

Women Returners, a coaching, consulting and networking organisation, pioneered the introduction of returnship programmes into the UK. Julianne Miles, co-founder and Managing Director, talked to us about their value and relevance:

"Returnships work well for people who would value a trial period," she explained. "This may be to try out a new sector or a different way of using your skills and experience, or simply to test whether it's the right time to return to work.

"It's tied in with confidence," she continued. "We come across many women who've had a long career break and they're anxious about going back. They're concerned about going into a role that's going to stretch them and they don't want to let people down. So they target roles below their skill set. Which is a waste of their abilities and often leads to them being frustrated within a short period of time when their confidence returns.

"Returnships give them time to transition back to work. With no pressure to perform from day one and with access to a coach, women usually find that they are perfectly able to go back and take on roles at a senior level and with plenty of responsibility."

These programmes are growing in popularity in the UK and have been used in industries as diverse as construction and financial services, with O2, Skanska, Tideway, Fidelity, PwC and Deloitte being amongst companies that regularly offer opportunities. LinkedIn began its own programme, 'ReturnIn' in 2018.

Judith Bradbury, Virgin Money ReCareer Programe

Judith spoke to us four months into her role with Virgin Money, where she joined their inaugural ReCareer programme. She is passionate and enthusiastic about the opportunity the scheme afforded her and keen to share her story.

Judith returned after a 12-year break. You read that correctly. 12 years.

Her early career was in banking, including a stint working in Germany, and had culminated in her co-founding a fuel cell technology start up. Her role there included everything from writing the business plan, to creating the website, writing contracts and undertaking three successful funding rounds. When the business was taken over it had over 70 employees in three countries. The takeover left Judith unexpectedly without a job for the first time.

Life moves on. She had children, moved to the Middle East for her husband's job, moved back to a small town in Northumberland, and before she knew it realised she was about to hit 50 (happens to us all). It was time to go back to work.

"It suddenly hit me that it was now or never. I'd qualified as a Corporate Treasurer, done an MBA, achieved Chartered Institute of Marketing qualifications, gained global business experience and I spoke several languages. I'd always been career focused, I thought, what a waste," she told us.

She had a few thwarted attempts at applying for locally

advertised jobs, including an operations manager maternity cover for an arts centre, and an internal communications role at Siemens. When nothing came of these attempts, she found herself questioning whether her skills were still relevant. She then came across the Virgin Money ReCareer programme.

"I did a little dance of joy!" she exclaimed. "Virgin Money have a reputation for thinking differently and doing things that aren't the norm. They were prepared to take me at face value – they didn't dismiss me out of hand because of that 12-year career gap."

Judith joined what was originally designed to be a 13-week internship style programme and was soon offered a senior role.

"Virgin Money arranged for me to meet people from two different departments, one of which offered me a permanent role. They're confident I can do the job, I have a fantastic line manager who is really supportive and although it's been a huge learning experience I'm totally loving it," she told us.

We asked Judith why the ReCareer programme was more effective for her than simply finding a job through a traditional route.

"Being part of a cohort," she answered. "We all started together, so there are people you can go to who are in the same situation, asking similar questions. We've formed strong bonds and support each other through all the challenges, both at home and at work."

SPECIALIST RECRUITERS AND JOBS BOARDS

Returnships are a welcome addition to the scene as they shine a light on this opportunity. They are not a magic bullet; they tend to happen once a year and can only have capacity for a relatively small number of women, but they are growing in popularity across several sectors. Happily, they are not the only route back. Some recruiters, such as Inclusivity Partners and The Return Hub focus on finding places for people coming back after a break.

The Return Hub

Dominie Moss has a background in executive search for Financial Services. She set up The Return Hub in 2016: more and more of her clients were looking for women and just couldn't find them. With over 15 years in the business, Dominie was well aware of the problem. And the opportunity.

"It felt as though we were at a time in history when there was a chance to do something different. For the first time, there were large numbers of professionally educated women, who'd had their children slightly later, in their thirties, who therefore had a good 10 to 15 years' experience before they took a break," she explained.

"And that meant that when they were ready to come back, they had a good 20 years ahead to continue their career."

Convinced that this was a viable business opportunity and, more importantly, fired up with frustration at seeing so many talented women shut out from the workplace, Dominie set up *The Return Hub* .

The Return Hub specialises in connecting employers with financial services professionals who have been on a career break. Dominie works with clients to ensure the right support is put around the candidate, be that through coaching, mentoring or training of line managers.

"Every time I have any doubts about this business – and there are many – all I have to do is think back to the women I see around the table when I run a workshop. They are such talented, impressive women. I know that when businesses see what I see they will get it. This is a high value proposition."

Michelle's story

Michelle had a varied career in Financial Services, working in investment management, consultancy and for the regulator, before taking a step back after she gave birth to twin girls. Rather than return to the city, she found a role closer to home, working for an independent investment management practice.

"It was supposed to be a stop gap role," she told us. "I ended up staying for 4 years."

Working 3 days a week, Michelle helped the founder grow the business: she took on the role of operations manager, setting up a client relationship management system and organising marketing and recruiting activities.

On the one hand, life was perfect. She was able to fit in work around her childcare. And yet Michelle began to feel as though it was time to step back up, ready to move on. In her words "I was ready for something more challenging.

I wanted to be back on the scene."

She approached several recruiters, most of whom wanted to know what she had been doing in the last 6 months. When she explained that her recent experience wasn't representative of the bigger picture, they disengaged. And that was even before she raised the possibility of flexible working.

Michelle took a step back. She thought about what she was good at and enjoyed and the value she could add to any organisation operating in the field of investment management and financial advice. She created her 'pitch'.

"Michelle is an experienced professional with deep client relationship management skills and 15 years track record in investment management and financial advice. She is highly tuned to the needs of high net-worth clients and understands the regulatory environment of this sector. Having worked with both large and small organisations, she is a highly pragmatic, experienced operator who is looking for a new role helping to shape and grow a business in this sector."

Michelle invested time in rebuilding her networks. It took time and effort. Eventually, Dominie introduced her to a woman running a new type of investment fund, who needed someone with just her skill set. Michelle is now back at work; her career is progressing once more and she still has the flexibility she needs to share parenting responsibilities equally with her partner.

There's a burgeoning market in companies who advertise part time and flexible roles. **Timewise, MumsNet Jobs** and **Capability Jane** are three very established sites.

At the risk of alienating so many hard-working people (often women) who are driving these businesses with such passion and determination, we won't pretend we can offer an exhaustive list.

Suffice to say they are there, ready and waiting. Some have a national reach while others hone in on a specific sector. Companies such as **Ten2Two** focus on a particular geographic area with local offices in the south of England, specialising in local employers for local candidates.

2to3days, on the other hand, is an online platform which matches and connects employers with mothers who can input their skills and how many hours they are looking to work.

TAILORED CONTRACTS

In some cases, the biggest barrier to women returning is the lack of roles with a high level of flexibility. Women might want to work no more than three days a week, or within hours that fit with school hours both of which are hard to accommodate in many organisations.

AMV BBDO, the creative agency, recently launched an innovate scheme to hire 10 'half-time' permanent roles to its creative department. The scheme is aimed at wooing female creative talent who feel unable to return because of the time commitment required.

Flexibility is built in a contractual level – women work around half the working hours required in standard employment contracts, which will usually mean 3.5 hours per day instead of 7 hours. The women receive the same type of creative briefs to work on, training and appraisals as full-time employees.

"There are plenty of 'returnships' run by agencies, which let women returning from a career break gain invaluable experience, but they don't go far enough in changing the fundamentals. The point of this programme is to give parents and care givers permanent positions within our creative department with flexibility built in at a contractual level." Ian Pearman, AMV BBDO

INDUSTRY AND SECTOR INITIATIVES

In addition, there are a number of different initiatives in certain sectors and in individual organisations to support the needs of people returning after a long break. The Daphne Jackson Fellowship, for example, is a funded programme to support people who want to go back to research careers, usually in the STEM field. Creative Equals offer a 'Making A Creative Comeback' programme aimed at female creative talent in the advertising industry; and F1 Recruitment run an annual 'Back2Businessship' intensive 6 day programme for PR, marketing and communications professionals.

Added to this, many individual companies now offer events for women in their sector, focusing on practical skills such as CV writing, using Linkedin and interviewing techniques. For example, Bloomberg invite applications for their annual Returner Circles where participants can be brought up to speed on the business is now and receive specialist coaching.

Many excellent professional bodies, such as the ICAEW for accountants run training programmes designed to help people who've had a break There are a wealth of opportunities to get out there, be seen, learn and become a little more match fit. Do some digging, look at the professional body for your sector, if there is one; keep an eye on large organisations that are committed to providing more opportunities for women. The good news is so many people are taking some tangible action to help.

Checklist for this Chapter

✓ Are you tracking returnships relevant to your sector or competency set?

✓ Have you registered with the job sites and jobs boards relevant to you?

✓ Have you identified any support programmes offered by your industry body?

✓ Are you following some of your targeted organisations to understand any courses or events on offer?

✓ Have you made contact with any specialist recruiters who could help?

Resources

candidates.capabilityjane.com

inclusivity.co.uk

Jobs.mumsnet.com

thereturnhub.com

ten2two.org

timewisejobs.co.uk

womenreturners.com

C. BACK WITH A DIFFERENCE: PORTFOLIO CAREERS

In this section, we will clarify what we mean by a 'portfolio career' and provide examples of organisations that are helping you access relevant skills and advice.

Returning to your old industry may feel dull or stifling – you may have multiple projects or three or four ideas you want to pursue. Perhaps some freelancing, dipping your toe into a startup or small consultancy, offering services voluntarily or finally pursuing further training or that longed for creative dream. You may have desire to write, join a board or secure a non-executive position.

A portfolio career can be a viable option. In fact, this approach to work is now seen as aspirational by many who are making a conscious decision to deploy their skills and experience across a number of organisations – often a mix of voluntary and paid activity.

Section 3 – If Not Now, When – discusses how changes to technology mean that it is now more possible than ever to set up your own business and to work wherever and whenever you want. The gig economy makes it easier to take your skills to market in a flexible way and though new business models have some disadvantages, particularly in terms of security of employment, they do work well for lots of people.

"I have found a zero hours contract to be a fantastic way to ensure flexibility ...I am able to work when I want, but I do not have the stress if my children are ill and I need to take time off."

The benefits can be incredible. Moving between different projects and organisations can be both energising and motivating. The insight you gain can be cross-referenced and your network expands. A portfolio career can open your eyes, taking you away from the often myopic view of one organisation.

We're not naive and acknowledge this is no utopia. Some freelance or interim agencies can be as sniffy about career gaps as large recruiters. Non-executive board seats are not that easy to land. It's a temptation to fill the diary full of potentially fun and exciting speaking opportunities, coffees, consulting projects, sales meetings. Proposals can take months to evolve, and often fall at the last hurdle. Payment terms can be sticky – you may take longer to acquire a regular income.

But equally, building a portfolio you find enriching, that deploys all of your skills and passions, can feel like it's the only way to work.

Compared to having a 'regular' job, building a portfolio career probably requires even more commitment and discipline. And the likelihood is that if you weren't self-employed before, you're going to need to upskill in a number of key areas. The good news is that there are plenty of businesses and free tools that can help.

We don't profess to offer a comprehensive list, but there are a few great examples that illustrate the type of support on offer.

Digital Mums Digital Mums was set up by Nikki Cochrane and Kathryn Tyler when they recognised the commercial opportunity to upskill mums in social media management.

"We started to think about what makes a good social media manager – someone who's level headed, a good communicator, who can multitask – and we began to realise that we were actually describing mums," Cochrane told us.

Social media can be managed remotely with technology allowing people to schedule tweets and Facebook posts in advance and to monitor different platforms on the go. Neither Cochrane or Tyler are mums themselves, but they knew plenty of women who were struggling to combine work and a family.

Their core business trains women to become social media managers through a 24-week remote education programme which takes between 10 to 15 hours a week, and includes 'on the job' training, designing campaigns for real clients, working to a live brief.

Their new Digital Retox programme focuses on the digital technologies crucial to the modern workplace. It covers topics such as big data, the benefits of cloud technologies, workflow automation and the use of collaborative working tools.

At times, we know it's not the length of a career break that's a problem, it's what's happened during that break in the rapidly evolving world of work. This programme aims to close some key knowledge gaps.

Cochrane and Tyler have a strong sense of purpose around helping women find meaningful, rewarding work that can fit around the rest of their lives. They campaign for more flexible working opportunities with initiatives such as their #WorkThatWorks Movement and #CleanUpTheFWord campaign; and 10% of their profits go to a bursary fund to enable women on low incomes to gain access to their training.

Talented Ladies Club is an online community for mothers who are ambitious to do more with their talents and time. Established by Hannah Martin and Kary Fisher, their magazine style website has over 1,800 live online articles on everything from marketing, PR, strategy and salary negotiations, to psychology, relationships, wellbeing and style – they publish fresh content daily.

They also run a lively Facebook community for entrepreneurial mothers and a growing library of popular online courses covering everything from writing your CV and LinkedIn profile to mastering Twitter and launching a profitable business. Their Kickstarter Course is designed to guide people through their first year in business.

Hannah explains: "It's really important to me that we take mothers through a practical, sequenced programme with plenty of support as they embark on their business journey – and that they actually make money."

Mums Enterprise are organisers of the Mums Enterprise Roadshow, a free to attend child-friendly, flexible work and business show offering support, advice and opportunities for those wanting to retrain, find flexible work, start or grow a business. Founded by Lindsey Fish and Lucy Chaplin, the duo began with two small regional shows in 2016. Events have since grown into large scale national exhibitions attracting thousands of women to each.

It's worth repeating that whilst there are more opportunities to develop portfolio careers and a range of places to go for help, working like this can be just as exhausting and stressful – if not more so – than being in permanent employment.

Be clear on why you have decided to work like this, how much time you are prepared to give and where the money is going to come from. Identify the skills and experience you're going to need and the investment it could take before offering your products or services. Who are you expecting to sell to? How will you take it to market? How will you sustain different parts of the portfolio?

The tactics we have described elsewhere in this book – getting your story straight, building a network, creating a powerful LinkedIn profile – are just as relevant if you decide that a portfolio career is for you.

Building a Portfolio Career – Jenny Cowderoy

We'd like to leave you with the story of Jenny, who began her working life above a pet shop in Leeds. 20-odd years later, she has a successful portfolio career which allows her to fulfil her professional ambitions, spend a decent amount of time with her children and also tap in to her creative side.

When Jenny recounted her story, it struck us that, unwittingly, she had taken many of the actions we advocate in this book.

Jenny's career began accidentally. After a postgraduate course in publishing, she stumbled into a tiny digital agency in Leeds in 1998. The work appeared interesting, fresh and creative. No-one, at the time, really had any idea what digital meant – building websites felt totally pioneering, frontier stuff. Jenny recalls printing and faxing website designs to clients, with a vague idea that they might one day take off. The business expanded very quickly, eventually taking up residence in the NatWest tower in London.

Then came 2001: share prices crashed, the digital marketing industry went, as Jenny described it, "tits-up", all agencies downsized. Her company promptly made most of their staff redundant.

Out of a job and with bills to pay, Jenny took a step back. She thought about her skills and strengths – what she had to offer to employers – brushed up her CV and began to sell her story. Highlighting the value of her unusual skill set, she pivoted one step, landing a role at GSK, where she later became Global Director for Digital Marketing.

In that role, she met regularly with Google, who were expanding rapidly. In a world full of young, male techies, Jenny stood out – she was client friendly, didn't do jargon and had a warm, calm, highly engaging manner. Google snapped her up to be their Head of Healthcare and FMCG.

During her seven years there, she had two children. Returning after her second maternity leave, she found her working world had changed – something that happens to many women. Google had new products, a new structure, a new senior team and Jenny was offered a new role. She had to make a decision. Stay or go.

Uncertain about what she really wanted, she invested in a personal coaching, which helped her think things through properly and with perspective.

"I was able to create a vision for my long-term future. I realised that fighting for this job would require sacrifices and that it wouldn't get me to where I ultimately wanted to be. Although I love challenge and change, I wasn't really sure how much I wanted it anymore. felt like a huge risk but I knew I had to leave."

Jenny's long-term vision was to have a portfolio career, running a boutique digital consultancy, a handful of board and non-executive roles, some free time for a creative activity, and flexibility around her children. Seductive and compelling but was it attainable? As the major breadwinner in the family, she didn't have the luxury of time.

"I was so driven, and felt I was taking control of my work life, for the first time ever, and this was my choice about my career. I grew up in a working-class family so financial security and status were important to me. The fear and risk of this not working drove me on."

Stepping back, Jenny created a road map, which included relocating to Bath, a creative city with relatively easy access to both London and Bristol, a growing centre of technology. It gave her access to a rich network of potential clients as well as offering a different family lifestyle. She knew she was competing in a world dominated by young men but drew confidence from knowing that she was a woman with plenty of experience and networks, which she quickly mobilised to build a portfolio of work. A couple of interim CEO roles enabled her to plug the gap of senior leadership experience.

Fine art has become what Jenny describes as the missing piece in the jigsaw. One day each week is devoted to the development of her craft as a fine artist, specialising in the Japanese aesthetic of Wabi-sabi. Systematic as ever, Jenny worked towards an exhibition, built a website and has an agent who helps her to sell her exquisite paintings.

By pausing, playing the long game, shaping a vision, formulating a plan, skilling up and eventually following her passion, Jenny's current contented state shines through when you meet her. Her current portfolio grows by the week – she's a woman in demand, with lucrative and enjoyable roles in several independent consultancies and companies. Her art is gorgeous too.

"I feel stepping away allowed me to swap a corporate job for a whole lifestyle. I work harder but I'm busier and happier than I've ever been. I work with many different associates and I'm building a great virtual team I support my family and I can be flexible around my kids."

Jenny, you're a marvel.

Other Resources

Books

My Creative (Side) Business: The insightful guide to turning your side projects into a full-time creative business: Volume 2 (Insightful Guides for Freelancers) by Monika Kanokova

The 4-Hour Work Week: Escape the 9-5, Live Anywhere and Join the New Rich by Tim Ferris

The Start Up of You: Adapt to the Future, Invest in Yourself and Transform your Career by Reid Hoffman

Websites

digitalmums.com
mumsenterprise.events
talentedladiesclub.com
jennycowderoy.com

7

The F word – flexibility

We know that flexibility is the number one ask for women looking to reignite their careers. And not just for women. Millennials, men and many of us, frankly, want to have some balance in our lives. To quote Arianna Huffington:

> **"**We're suffering from the delusion that in order to succeed we need to burnout ... In order to be most creative, most productive, we need to prioritise our own ability to recharge.**"**

Arianna's new business – Thrive Global – is about helping individuals and organisations change this culture through solutions to enhance well-being, performance and purpose. Addressing the culture of long hours and presenteeism, and embracing more balanced, flexible working patterns is an essential part of that change.

This chapter covers:

- What we mean by flexibility
- Why is it so important

- How to negotiate what you need
- Setting boundaries and making your time count

WHAT WE MEAN BY FLEXIBILITY

Many organisations have different terms – Agile and Dynamic being the most common. Semantics aside, let's be clear what we're talking about here: put simply, it's about *where, when* and *how much* work gets done.

Where – in an office, at home or in some other space

When – 9 to 5, for 48 weeks a year, at the same time as everyone else, at times of your choosing, or somewhere in between

How much – How many hours of work do you actually do

We spoke to Karen Mattison, joint CEO of Timewise, the flexible working experts, about the changes she has seen over the last 10 years.

"Huge leaps and bounds have been made on the where and the when," she explained, going on to talk about the opportunities offered by technology as well as the commercial drive all companies are facing to minimise expensive real estate costs whilst at the same time operating 24/7.

"How much? That's still a sticking point. It's an uncomfortable truth for many organisations that most people want to work fewer hours. Our most recent research proves that one in four full time workers want this. At Timewise, we believe that what's needed is a truly flexible jobs market. For everyone."

Flexible working arrangements encompass many different arrangements, including:

- Compressed hours (for example, doing full time hours but in fewer days a week)
- Term time only working.
- Annualised hours contracts (where you work more hours some weeks, less in others, providing the total over the year adds up).
- Flexible hours (usually flexibility over your start and finish times).
- Part time working.
- Job Sharing.
- The option to work wholly or partly from home
- Shift work.

WHY IS FLEXIBILITY SO IMPORTANT?

The reasons people want and need flexibility are varied and could include:

- Time for further study
- Personal health reasons
- Writing a book
- Being on a glide path to retirement
- Starting a new business
- Being involved in a charity
- Taking on a voluntary position

- Training for a sporting event
- Fitting work around children
- Caring responsibilities

We have met so many people in different situations who are asking for a change from the norm. For example, Claire Moyne, Director of HR for Edo Digital Consultancy in Bristol has set her sights on becoming one of the top 5 amateur triathletes in UK for and is negotiating time off around her intense training programme, working twice daily with a professional coach.

In a different sector completely, Jeff is an experienced tunnel engineer and would love to continue to work on the HS2 project, but as he approaches retirement wants to scale down to three days a week. He is an invaluable mentor to younger, well-trained but less experienced engineers.

It's not just about women with children, neither is it simply relevant for lower level roles. Timewise run an annual award programme – the Timewise Power 50 List – which highlights and celebrates people from different fields adopting different types of flexible working. The 2017 list included Anushka Asthana and Heather Stewart who job share the role of political editor of the Guardian, and men and women doing senior roles across a range of sectors on a part-time basis.

Flexibility is important – people want it and it makes business sense. And yet Timewise's own research shows that only 10% of 'quality' jobs (which they define as paying over £20k per annum) advertised in the UK mention any form of flexibility. Demand far outstrips supply.

Which means that whether you are in a job now and would like more balance or are looking for a new job and want flexibility in your working arrangements, you're probably going to need to negotiate it.

HOW TO NEGOTIATE FLEXIBILITY

Here are some pointers. Some are more relevant to a totally new role, others if you are asking to change your current working arrangements.

- **Do your homework.**

Find out whether the company you're interviewing with already offers flexibility. If there are no precedents elsewhere in the organisation, and the role is not being advertised as being flexible it might be better to focus your efforts elsewhere. If the company is winning awards, the opposite may be true.

- **Focus first and foremost on your role and what you will deliver.**

Get the job first. Paint a picture of success. Focus on your role, what you will deliver and why you're perfect for it. Why you are confident it can be delivered in that way. If you have examples from a previous role, use them. Don't start the conversation with why you need flexibility. Who cares, apart from you, that you need to collect children from school at 4pm on a Thursday.

A flexible solution for the British Chambers of Commerce

Dr Adam Marshall, Director General of the British Chambers of Commerce, wanted to revitalise the brand. He needed the right expertise and the ability to navigate 52 chambers across the country. At the same time, the role didn't need – and the budget wouldn't allow – a full time senior person.

We introduced Adam to Lucy, who was looking for a part time role. Their discussions centred on where Adam wanted to take the brand, the alternative strategies to get there and how Lucy would approach the task.

"I was sure I could deliver what they were after," Lucy told us.

When the conversation finally turned to working hours, Lucy had already painted a picture of how she could help them. She then suggested:

"I can start three weeks on Tuesday. I will work all day Tuesday, a half day on Wednesday and all day Friday. And I can be flexible on that provided you give me some notice".

Sold on Lucy doing the role, her hours of work were much less of an issue. She made it easy for the team to say yes. As a result, the BCC now has an experienced marketer on the team, who is not only helping shape and deliver their brand strategy but is also a great mentor to junior members.

- **Build a business case.**

Many organisations now recognise the economic value of
enabling people to work remotely, be that from home or
other locations. Fewer have cottoned on to the fact that
there can also be a business benefit to having more people
working flexible – and sometimes reduced – hours.

Why does it make sense for the company to take you on
a flexible arrangement? If you're going to work 4 days a
week, will the cost be 80% of what it would have been to
hire someone 5 days a week? Where else could that money
be invested? The BCC could not afford Lucy full time. She
was a cost-effective hire. They have someone with expertise,
efficiency, stability and enthusiasm delivering efficiently in
the time she is there.

Be clear about the benefit *to the business* of you working in
this way.

- **Be the Solution, not the Problem and be flexible yourself.**

Present yourself as open and solutions focused. If you are
asking your employer for flexibility, be realistic about the
needs of the business and negotiate an arrangement that
suits all parties. If your starting request is rigid, you're adding
to this person's problems. Don't – they have enough already.

If in doubt, suggest a trial period

- **Nail the detail.**

How many hours you work and the expectations of your
delivery within those hours is critical. The temptation is to be
overjoyed at having landed a reduced hours role. The devil
is in the detail here. On both sides. Have you clarified and

agreed job design, how this role will be measured, targets, how work will be done and how any people management responsibilities are allocated.

Bear in mind it's not simply your own role that will be affected, it could also be the number of clients you're responsible for, the number of direct reports you have to look after, the number of internal projects or initiatives you get involved with. Each of these will have a demand on your time.

The business needs to be just as clear on how this will work as you.

● **Work within the system.**

If you have been with an employer for 26 weeks or more, you have a right to request flexible working. Take time to understand what their formal process is for making that request. Our advice would be to discuss and negotiate what you're looking for in conversations – bearing in mind the business needs – and then use this process to rubber stamp what's been agreed. Where people put in a request that doesn't fully consider the business side, and which hasn't had buy in from line managers, they are surprised when it is turned down.

● **Be ready for the objections.**

The person hiring you will have to manage risk. What objections could they encounter?

"Someone else will have to pick up the slack."

"The rest of the team are going to feel resentful."

"What if everyone suddenly wants it?"

"What about clients who demand a response 24/7?"

Have you suggested how you communicate your role with the team, how you manage handovers, who takes over as the client contact point when you're not there? Demonstrate that you have thought about the questions and have a plan to deal with them once you start.

- **Identify the development opportunities for others.**

Reducing your working hours could offer development opportunities for others. This could form part of your responses to the objections raised above.

Lucy, above, identified that there were some junior people on the team, who she would be able to train up to take on some extra responsibilities and thus be cover on the days she wasn't there.

- **Make your career ambitions part of the conversation.**

Part-time need not mean unambitious. Make this clear by talking not only about how you will perform this role but also where you see your career going next.

Stop talking about your hours, talk about your ambition

Emily works for PwC in a sales and marketing role, developing propositions for large government sector and blue chip clients. She took on this role, working 4 days a week, when returning from her second maternity leave.

When her youngest son was offered a place at nursery between 9am and 4pm she thought her career ambitions were over. Even a 4-day week looked impossible. Luckily, her mum intervened.

"Why not just work it differently?"

Emily did her homework. She studied the firm's policy and also took time to talk to her business sponsor about her proposal – to spread her 80% hours over 5 days, with a combination of hours in the office and hours working at home. She reiterated her excitement, commitment and confidence in her ability to deliver the role.

Preparation proved critical. When her proposal was initially rejected because it didn't appear to fit with policy she was able to politely suggest management look closer. The second objection that 'it may not work for the business' fell away when her sponsor backed her up, saying "I'm confident she can make it work."

The firm agreed a three-month trial, after which this new arrangement became permanent.

We asked Emily what she felt was key to success:

"One of the first things I did was be totally transparent with the rest of the team about my working hours" she explained. "I marked out on my calendar my office hours, hours working at home, and hours when I was non-contactable, save for an emergency. And I also asked for people to contact me by text if there were any emergencies."

Emily spoke to another woman who she knew had made partner on 3 days a week, who gave her an invaluable piece of advice:

> **"**Stop talking about your need for flexibility and talk instead about your ambition.**"**

"That was a turning point," she says. "I know I can do this job, this way. I feel set free. This IS full time for me, I don't need to do any more hours than this. I'm far more efficient now than I ever was before I had my children. Previously, I used to think about what jobs I could do where I could work flexibly, now I am thinking about where I want to take my career next, knowing I'm just as good – if not better – than I ever was."

● Set yourself up to be successful

Do you have the right working environment and do you have the right technology – and tech support – including bandwidth at home? Have you sorted space where you know you can work without interruption? Have you talked to your family and anyone else who will be impacted about what you will need from them?

Do you have backup plans if anything goes wrong? If you're returning from a break where you have been the sole carer for children, it's likely you have been the first port of call if there have been any issues at school.

When Jenni went back to work as a teacher, having her phone on during lessons wasn't an option.

"My husband just had to take this on. We had to keep reminding the kids that I just was not contactable. At all. It was a blessing really because for the first 6 months I was on my knees and just couldn't have coped with anything other than getting on top of being in the job again."

Timewise have long been campaigning for the growth of the UK's quality part-time and flexible jobs market. They offer much advice for both employers and candidates, through their national jobs board *Timewise Jobs* . Take a look.

How a lawyer flexed down ... and up again

Sometimes, people are so sure that flexible working won't work they don't even ask. They look around and see no-one else doing it and don't even have the conversation about what might be possible.

At other times, women try hard to negotiate a flexible working solution only to find their requests fall on deaf ears. We love Laura's story because it worked the other way around. After struggling with managing a young family and a working day regularly spanning calls from 6am to 10pm, she felt she had to leave the firm, several times, only to be persuaded by her boss, Kirsty, that flexible working was the solution.

She was a lawyer working with a large firm when she decided she had to take a career break to look after two small children. Luckily Kirsty didn't want her to go and persuaded her instead to reduce her hours.

"I thought she'd go mad. I also thought she'd regret it," Kirsty explained.

Working in a similar role on a 3-day week, Laura felt frustrated that she couldn't give her best at home or at work. This pattern continued and in the end Kirsty adjusted Laura's role until Laura ended up doing just 20 hours a month for the firm, with a specific new project to manage. Less than one day a week.

A lot of thought went into the role and how Laura could add value. What this definitely achieved was to keep Laura connected with the firm. And with the idea of both working and being a mother. So that before too long she felt able to go back up to 2.5 days, one of which is from home.

When Lisa last met them, Laura was leading a successful team as a result of developing the project, with the support of the firm, into a new business area. She is now looking to increase her working days now that both children are at school and she's ready to go onto the partner track.

It's not always possible to be as flexible as Kirsty was in this situation – and we have found few other examples of this type of arrangement. However, if you can make it work it's such a win for both sides. Laura managed to keep hold of her career and not only does the firm retain a very talented woman, they can demonstrate to younger lawyers their commitment to retaining female talent.

SETTING BOUNDARIES

Success is not just about making the right arrangements on day one, it's also about making it work by putting the right boundaries in place.

If you and your employer approach the boundary conversation with the attitude "together we need to work out what's important and how we're going to make this role work", you're much more likely to arrive at an outcome which works for both parties.

What are your boundaries?

- Do you have any flexibility at all around days and hours of work?
- If so, do you need a certain amount of notice?
- When will you take calls, if at all, and from whom?
- When do team meetings take place and how (all face to face or dial in)?
- When can you be expected to check email?
- How will you ensure you have a hard stop on your working day, if you need it?
- How will you use online tools such as a shared calendar, your out of office notification etc, to let others know when you're not available?

Be honest about what you need, what's acceptable and what's not. Have a dialogue about it.

Whatever your official role description you are inevitably going to be asked to other things from time to time. They could be large, could be small.

Nanette Gartrell has written a very helpful book called *My Answer Is No If That's OK With You*, which we would thoroughly recommend. It takes a fresh look at why even the most powerful, accomplished, and successful women find it difficult to say NO, and offers a revolutionary approach to setting limits without jeopardizing important relationships.

There's good news too, though. Saying "No" politely and firmly doesn't mean you are disliked. It could even buy you respect if you do it in the right way. Gartrell suggests a six-point plan, which we will paraphrase:

- **Give yourself time:** Don't respond immediately. Tell the person asking you'll get back to them by a specific date or time, once you've checked out your schedule.

- **Weigh up the pros and cons**. What will you gain by saying no – control of your time, ability to focus on your own job, for example – and what could you lose. A relationship? Support for your own work in the future? Be realistic.

- **Does it fit with your own priorities and job description?** If the task can be done within the time you have available, and if it's aligned with your own job anyway, then saying yes might make sense. If not, then saying no could be the only way of you staying within the boundaries you've agreed for yourself.

- **Be firm with No**. People will take a clear No much better than a mushy "well, sorry, I'd love to but I just don't know, you see I have these deadlines to meet and I'm really not sure I could fit it in ......" – this just leaves the asker confused about what you're really saying and with the impression that you could be persuaded.

- **Offer brief explanation.** If and only if you feel it's needed. Otherwise you risk running into the mushiness of the example above.

- **Suggest alternatives.** The person asking you might just have asked you because they couldn't think of anyone else. Or you might have been the first person they bumped into. Or maybe you always say yes. Suggest someone else who might be able to do the job or for whom it could be a development opportunity. That way you're being helpful without committing your own time.

MAKE YOUR TIME COUNT

If you're going to deliver your objectives within the boundaries you're set, you're going to have to be ruthless about your time.

We asked women who'd taken career breaks which skills, if any, had improved during that time. 65% said they were far better at planning ahead and 60% felt their time management skills were sharper.

Use this in the workplace. We all know there is a huge amount of time wasting in organisations. We recently polled our network for their favourites:

- Conference calls that run late in the evening to get different country teams on board even when the decision has actually already been made.
- Emails that are cc'd to 9 or 10 different people.
- 360-degree performance appraisal processes that absorb hundreds of hours of people's time.
- A commute that would be 30 minutes faster if only I could do it an hour later.
- Perfection over excellence.

● Initiatives that go on forever because management can't make a decision.

Meeting your commitments at home and at work will only be possible if you're ruthless about time management.

Time management isn't simply about prioritising well, it's also about understanding what sort of environment you need to work productively, achieve flow and also how the pattern of your brain works. When are you most creative? When should you schedule low level tasks? When would you just be better taking a break and walking the dog?

There are some excellent resources to help with all of these, some of which are listed below. One of our favourites is *Rework: Change the way you work forever* by Jason Fried and David Heinemeier Hansson has been a real inspiration for us at She's Back. We love this quote:

> **"**Good enough is fine. When good enough gets the job done, go for it. It's way better than wasting resources or, even worse, doing nothing because you can't afford the complex solution. And remember, you can usually turn good enough into great later.**"**

Another classic is Stephen Covey's *Seven Habits of Highly Effective People*, one chapter of which – *Habit 3, Put First Things First* – sets out some obvious but often ignored rules about distinguishing between urgent and non-urgent, important and unimportant activities.

As technology continues to offer new opportunities, agile, dynamic, flexible working will become more and more prevalent. The task of negotiating what you need should, we hope, be a little easier. In the meantime, take confidence from everything you know about your ability to manage your time and deliver on your priorities in your personal life. It will be worth it.

Your Checklist for This Chapter

Have you:

✓ Established exactly what working patterns would work for you?

✓ Created a set of alternative scenarios that might fit with your needs?

✓ Identified what flexibility you have within those scenarios?

✓ Researched the policies and the current practices and precedents at your target or current employer?

✓ Clarified exactly what the role needs you to deliver?

✓ Provided evidence that you can deliver what's required in the manner you propose?

✓ Established a business case?

✓ Thought through any potential objections?

✓ Considered, specifically, the impact on external client service, if appropriate?

✓ Identified development opportunities for others?

✓ Nailed the detail of the role – targets, responsibilities?

✓ Discussed working boundaries and what support you will
 need?

✓ Agreed how to deal with emergencies or requests outside
 the norm?

Other Resources

Thrive: The Third Metric to Redefining Success and Creating a Happier Life by Arianna Huffington

Nice Girls Don't Get the Corner Office: the unconscious mistakes that women make that sabotage their careers by Lois P. Frankel

My Answer's No if that's Alright with you by Nanette Gartrell

Rework: Change the way you work forever by Jason Fried and David Heinemeier Hansson

The Way We're Working Isn't Working: The four forgotten needs that energize great performance by Tony Schwartz with Jean Gomes and Catherine McCarthy

How to be a Productivity Ninja by Graham Allcott.

Deep Work: rules for success in a distracted world by Cal Newport

7 Habits of Highly Effective People by Stephen Covey

8.

The other F word – finances

> **"**I really think the final or one of the final legs of feminism is for us to become financially equal with men. And putting it another way, until we are *financially* equal with men, we are not equal with men.**"**
>
> Sallie Krawcheck, CEO and Co-Founder Ellevest

Money is important. When we asked women who'd taken a break why they wanted to return, their first reason was personal fulfilment, followed very closely by money. We love this quote by Sallie Krawcheck because it's a stark reminder that if we want to achieve equality, financial equality has to be a part of that.

In this chapter we'll cover:

- Where women stand today
- How did we get here?
- Why is it so important to take back control?
- How and where do you start?

WOMEN AND MONEY: WHERE WE STAND TODAY

Let's start with some stark facts:

Women tend to earn less than men. There is a gender pay gap. Different reports will say different things about how big it is; academics, economists and business people will debate why it's there; but for our purposes, let's just accept that it's there.

Organisations in the UK employing more than 250 people now have to report on their gender pay gap as of February 2018. Many are reporting a gap of over 15% between men's mean hourly pay and that of women.

Women's pension pots are smaller – a fact less often reported, ergo much less discussed. It's also a bigger problem. Why? Because women are likely to live longer than men and therefore require more financial support during the later years of their lives.

In 2017, Mercer, the consultancy, found that the EU gender pension gap — measured by annual pension received and based on Eurostat data — was 40 per cent, compared to a gender pay gap of 16 per cent. There were wide variations between countries, with the gap ranging from 4 per cent to 49 percent. Half of the 28 EU members had a gap of 30 per cent or more.

Single parents. Increasingly the norm. Over 40% of marriages in the UK end in divorce and a report from the Chartered Insurance Institute in 2017 showed that a divorced woman on average had a pension pot worth a third of that of a divorced man. And that's if we get married at all: almost 50% of births in 2015 were outside marriage or civil partnership. Whilst that doesn't mean a partner isn't around at birth, that doesn't always remain the case throughout a child's life. The burden and cost of child rearing for divorced mothers and those who have never been married tends to fall disproportionately on the woman.

So here's the rub – we earn less, we save less and we bear an unequal share of the costs of childcare (and very probably the care of the elderly).

We spoke to Michelle Gyimah who works for the Equality and Human Rights Commission and has her own consulting business *Equality Pays*. Her business aims to help women learn how to control their money. Michelle set up the business after her personal experience of finding herself out of control financially.

"Money is always a difficult subject for people to talk about. It can often come loaded with a variety of emotions such as guilt, greed, fear, anger and if you look at the societal messaging around women and money it is even more loaded. Women are often derided or discouraged from talking about money or pursuing it in the same way as men.

"We teach our girls that the best attributes are kindness, sharing and nurturing, while our boys are taught to take risks, be brave, strong and 'go get em'. Whilst these lessons are not directly related to money, they are related to confidence and job choices which ultimately is related to money."

Michelle's view is that women need to acknowledge their emotions about money, get comfortable talking about it and develop some habits that will help them to become debt free and financially secure.

We concur. Yes, the system needs to change, and illegal pay discrimination has to be tackled. At the same time, we can't sit back and wait for that to happen. We need to take matters in hand.

HOW DID WE GET HERE?

When and how did we cede control over something so important? We are responsible human beings. It's not as though we don't understand the value of money. Mintel research in 2015 showed that 84% of mothers said they influenced family spending decisions, with only 49% saying their partner had influence. Other studies claim that women make 75% of all purchase decisions worldwide. It's not as if we can't add up.

We've identified 3 ways in which women get into this situation. There are undoubtedly many more, but here are our top 3:

1. We don't ask
2. We take career breaks without considering the impact on our long-term finances
3. We spend a lot of time doing a job that is unpaid and undervalued

We don't ask

Jennifer Lawrence summed it up when the Sony email hack revealed that she was being paid far less than her co-stars:

"When the Sony hack happened & I found out how much less I was being paid than the lucky people with dicks, I didn't get mad at Sony. I got mad at myself. I failed as a negotiator because I gave up early."

There is a lot of research out there that illustrates the many ways in which women don't ask. We don't ask for a pay rise out of turn, we don't ask for a promotion, we don't ask to be put on a high-profile project, we don't *ever* ask for special treatment unless we really have to. Instead we wait to be noticed. We do fantastic work; we're diligent; we play by the rules (because that is what we are taught) and we expect that the system will work. That those in power will see how brilliant and committed we are and the rewards will come our way.

That's not how it works.

In their book *Why Women Don't Ask* Linda Babcock and Sara Laschever unpack this brilliantly. For example, their research found that male graduates from a particular university were starting on salaries 7.6% higher than their female peers. Digging into the detail, they found that whilst only 7% of women had negotiated their starting salary offer, 57% of men (8 times as many) had done so.

Why does this matter so much? Imagine that from then on, all that everyone gets is a simple 3% pay rise each year. Over the course of a lifetime, that would be worth hundreds of thousands to the men because the difference compounds each year, not only for their salary but for their pension pots too.

They recall a powerful story of female grad students complaining that they weren't being given as many offers to teach that many of their male counterpart. Many of the men were being given 'proper' teaching slots whereas the women were being allocated roles as teaching assistants. When Linda delved into the problem it turned out that the men were actually asking for the teaching opportunities and the women were waiting for them to be offered.

Sound familiar?

To be sure there is discrimination out there, notwithstanding useful pieces of legislation like the Equal Pay Act and the new Gender Pay Gap Reporting Regulations. The point, though, is that it is not just up to businesses to close the pay gap. We too have a role to play.

We take career breaks without considering the personal financial impact on our long-term finances

Women are also much more likely than men to take a career break. Obviously, if you're not earning during that 6 month, or 1 year or 3 year break that has a financial impact. However, that's the tip of the iceberg when it comes to the havoc that a career break can have on your personal finances.

First, taking a career break can have a severe impact on someone's lifetime earnings potential. Sallie Krawcheck brought this to life in an article entitled *What a Career Break does to your Finances* with this example:

> Let's say Elle is a 30-year-old professional woman, earning $85,000 a year. She saves 20% of her salary and stashes it in the bank. She plans to take a 2-year career break in 5 years. When she returns, she takes a 20% pay cut. And it impacts her every year for the rest of her career, since she's getting raises off of a lower base.
>
> How much does this cost her, in aggregate earnings, over 40 years? $1.7 million. That's how much less she earns over that period of time.
>
> And where does this leave her as a grandma, when she retires? About $400,000 poorer.

In short, taking a pay cut for what might seem like a short amount of time actually sets you up to earn less money every year you are working, for the rest of your working life.

Let's say that again so it sticks...

Taking a pay cut for what might seem like a short amount of time actually sets you up to earn less money every year you are working, for the rest of your working life. Terrifying, isn't it?

Aside from this HUGE problem, taking a career break means that you potentially miss out on opportunities to contribute to a company pension scheme; participate in employee bonus schemes or long term incentive plans; benefit from access to employee share schemes; or simply cannot afford to take up these or other financial incentives. Again, like the salary cut, one you step away from some of these benefits, the risk is that you lose them forever.

We spend a long time doing a job that is unpaid and undervalued

Go back to the bright, ambitious, go-getting person you were at 22. Or even the mildly curious, "I need to work to pay for my social life" person you were at 22. Remember that person.

Could you imagine yourself signing up for a job that's 24 hours a day, 7 days a week, with no days off, no pay, no feedback (at least very little positive feedback), where you won't know you've really done a good job or not for 18 years or more.

Here's an advert, produced by Mullen Lowe back in 2014. It asks for applicants for such a job – the post of mother. It's obviously tongue in cheek and very funny but makes the point. It attracted 2.7million views but only 24 applicants: **https://youtu.be/HB3xM93rXbY**

Take someone whose had a relatively successful career, where they've had positive feedback, regular pay rises, promotions even, and put them into the role of a full-time mother for a few years – is it any wonder they come out lacking in the confidence to negotiate a great salary? Let alone go back to a reasonably senior level job.

The answer? Well, it's clearly not "stop being a parent". Neither is it "Don't take a career break". Instead, we'd encourage women to recognise their value, guard against complacency and take personal responsibility for their long term financial future.

TAKING BACK CONTROL

Educate yourself

The Financial Services industry is notoriously opaque but there are resources there to help and it's never as complicated as the so-called experts like to pretend. There are plenty of resources out there and we're no experts, so we won't recommend one over another. To make the point about simplicity, though, it's worth looking up the work of Harold Pollack, a University of Chicago public policy professor.

He was being interviewed about the financial advice industry and to make the point that Wall Street advice is overly complicated, he quickly grabbed an index card and jotted down nine basic financial rules that he and his wife had been living by. It was all you needed to know.

Pollack posted the card on his blog, and it quickly went viral, attracting hundreds of thousands of hits. Noted academics and pundits tweeted it out. Media outlets, including the *Washington Post* and *Money,* wrote stories about it.

Now that single card has morphed into a 240-page book, *The Index Card,* which explains in more detail why the rules work.

MAX your 401(k) or equivalent employee contribution,
Buy inexpensive, well-diversified mutual funds such as
Vanguard Target 20xx funds,
Never buy or sell an individual security. The person on the
other side of the table knows more than you do about this
stuff.
Save 20% of your money.
Pay your credit card balance in full every month.
Maximize tax-advantaged savings vehicles like Roth, SEP,
and 529 accounts.
Pay attention to fees. Avoid actively managed funds.
Make financial advisor commit to a fiduciary standard.
Promote social insurance programs to help people when
things go wrong.

Its basis is the US financial and tax system but many of the same rules apply. The point is not what they are, it's that they are actually reasonably straightforward.

There are many books devoted to educating women on how to maximise and manage their money so that they don't live in poverty after divorce or in old age. One important aspect that is often ignored, is the emotions and feelings that are unique to women around money. For many women, part of educating themselves around money lies in owning up to how they feel about money. The principles are not complicated – most advice covers a small number of well-worn and very true mantras:

- Set yourself some short, medium and long term financial goals
- Learn to budget
- Pay off debt

- Set up an emergency fund
- Get into the habit of saving
- Diversify your investments
- Maximise use of any tax efficient savings schemes
- Take full advantage of any pension contributions offered by your employer
- Find out if you're eligible for any childcare allowances, healthcare support or other benefits

Know your worth and learn to negotiate

> "You have to ask for things at work — women sit there waiting for things to come to them and not realising that actually all the men are running off asking for them. Things don't just happen, you don't get something because you sit politely and are well behaved — that's not how it works."
> Emily Maitliss

There are plenty of websites that give you information about the market rate for the job you're looking for, including *GlassDoor* and *Total Jobs* in the UK and *Comparably* in the US. Once you're there, ask for clarity around how future pay increases will be determined. Establish the clear, measurable, tangible goals that will set you up for future rewards, be they salary increases or bonuses.

If you are freelance or self-employed, beware giving away

your expertise for free. Have a rate card so that you can manage expectations and be transparent. Beware all those nice people asking to buy you a coffee to pick your brain.

Read *No You Can't Pick My Brain it Costs Too Much* by Adrienne Graham. What began as a blog post became so popular that Graham turned it into a book which is full of practical advice about how to determine your value and position yourself as an expert without spending an inordinate amount of time doing free consulting.

Reframe that childcare cost equation

Shared parental leave was introduced in the UK in April 2015, but as of January 2018 fewer than 2% of eligible couples had taken up the opportunity. We would love to see this trend change but in the meantime it remains the norm for women to take time away from work to look after young children.

And as a result, when couples start to think about childcare costs, they compare those costs to the mother's earnings, which can lead to this commonly heard refrain:

"By the time I've paid my childcare costs, it's hardly worth me going back to work."

Since when did any child only have one parent? Why do the equation like this, unless you are a one parent family? For every year that anyone takes out of work, their ability to return and their perceived value to an employer drops disproportionately. Not only should childcare costs be compared to the income of the whole household, this is one equation that should definitely take in a long-term view.

Be Strategic When Asking "Is it Worth it?"

We recently met a woman considering returning to a part-time role, who was pondering whether it was worth it, financially. The salary being offered was a fair amount less than she was earning before her break. At the time we spoke, her option was to earn nothing or take a job that would pay £24k per year. She was 40.

Let's say she took that role, with no pay increases, for the next 25 years, and saved 75% every month. Even assuming an interest rate of only 2.5%, in 25 years her savings would be over £625,000. That's a lot more than nothing.

> "Compound interest is the eighth wonder of the world. He who understands it, earns it ... he who doesn't ... pays it." Albert Einstein

Clearly, there's a lot more to factor into a decision about whether a salary offer is fair or worth it to you as an individual – including, of course, the prospect of future salary increases, bonuses and a subsequent move to a better paid job. The point, though, is to think long-term.

Think beyond cash

This may seem ironic in a chapter that is all about taking control of your finances but bear with us. There are other benefits on offer that could be of just as much value to you.

If you're in work and your employer can't meet your request for a pay rise, for example, think about what else they could do instead. Extra holiday, access to specific training, being assigned a mentor, payment of membership fees for a particularly valuable network, the opportunity to lead a specific project – all of these could well be of just as much value to you as cold hard cash. Be prepared to ask. People do generally like to say "yes" at some point during any negotiation.

Equally, if you're freelance or self-employed, be creative about thinking about how others could reward you for your support and advice. Again, cash isn't always the answer.

Early on in the life of She's Back, we needed sponsorship and support for a research project. One of our partners was able to offer the use of a stunning space overlooking the Thames for our launch event. Space that would have cost us the whole of our research budget.

Remember: most important of all no-one is going to do this for you. No one.

Take control. Today. People can help. Good luck.

Other Resources

Why Women Don't Ask by Linda Babcock and Sara Laschever

No, You Can't Pick My Brain, it Costs Too Much by Adrienne Graham

The Index Card: Why Personal Finance doesn't have to be complicated by Helaine Olen & Harold Pollack

You're a Badass at Making Money: Master the mindset of wealth by Jen Sincero

Money is Emotional: Prevent your heart from hijacking your wallet by Christine Luken

9.

Staying back

You've decided it's time to return, clarified what you want to do, told your network and found a job. Brilliant. Well done. Crack open the champagne.

We're pretty sure that you'll be feeling incredibly excited, anticipating the joy of some mental stimulation, spending the day interacting with other adults, rediscovering your professional self, dressing up for work, having a cup of tea at your desk in peace. And yet we also know that reality kicks in pretty quickly, when you get to grips with what you actually have to do.

It's a transition, there will be bumps along the way. EVERYONE goes through this. This transition phase, of establishing a 'new normal' can take 3 to 6 months, if not more. Don't worry but do be prepared. Forewarned is forearmed.

In this chapter we will:

● Explore the challenges of not just going back but then staying back.

● Suggest some practical strategies and tactics to ensure success.

- Explore the emotional ups and downs that come with this journey.

THE CHALLENGES OF STAYING BACK...

... are varied: the need to update your skills; having the right support on re-entry; mobilising the support systems you need at home, getting used to the new demands on your time...

It's a transformational change. Yet whilst there is a raft of advice on how organisations should deal with change, we haven't come across much which addresses the needs of someone returning to work. So, we will steal shamelessly from the works of major thinkers around organisational change and extract some useful advice.

The first is John P. Kotter, who wrote a seminal article for HBR called *Leading Change: Why Transformation Efforts Fail.*

Kotter cites 8 errors which lead to transformation efforts failing:

- Not establishing a great enough sense of urgency.
- Not creating a powerful enough guiding coalition.
- Lacking a vision.
- Under-communicating the vision by a factor of 10.
- Not removing obstacles to the new vision.
- Not systematically planning for and creating short term wins.
- Declaring victory too soon.
- Not anchoring changes in the corporation's culture.

Fear not, we are not about to crowbar the reasons why your return to work might be an unmitigated disaster into those 8 factors. Instead, we thought about all the stories people had told us and compared them to Kotter's headings. Since we prefer to look on the positive side, rather than dwell on reasons for failure, we focus on what will make your return a success.

1. Don't worry about achieving your dream immediately

After a 12-year break Sally wanted to return to work as a full-time office manager and landed an offer. Reluctantly, she turned it down when she realised that, with her daughters entering exam years and a partner who could often be working abroad for 3-month stints, it wasn't the right thing to do.

Longer term that might be what she wants, but this wasn't her vision for this year. So, she's working part time as an office manager at a fitness studio. It's a step on the way.

Advice: Be clear and honest. Think it through. Don't bite off more than you can chew. Be aware that your first role might not be where you end up. You may, instead need a number of stepping stones to get you to where you ultimately want to be.

2. Be clear about what's expected

Abi, an experienced sales and business development manager, secured a fantastic role at a startup online media company, following a 10-year break. She was an ideal fit as they needed to broker new advertising and sponsorship deals; her previous contacts, experience and negotiation skills meant she was well placed to help.

6 months into the role Abi chose to leave. Whilst she was very comfortable with sales and relationship development, she was less comfortable with the nuts and bolts of setting up an online campaign, using analytics and optimising digital channels. Too much was new. This was a start-up. Everyone was fantastic but slammed, no one had time to support or mentor her on the job. Abi retrained with Digital Mums – she stepped back to step up again. She's now taking on independent projects and testing her new skills. When she goes for her next role, she will be able to hit the ground running.

Advice: Spend time understanding the detail. Not just what the output and objectives will be, but what's the working environment going to be like. What skills and knowledge are you expected to have? Do you have them and if not, will the support be there?

3. Beware an alien environment

Rashmi had a 20-year career in financial services and IT delivery behind her, plus an MBA from Insead. She was delighted to be offered a place on a 12-week returnship programme with a bank. She was less delighted that her team at the bank appeared to feel resentful of her arrangement to leave early on a Thursday.

"I lasted 6 weeks but the atmosphere was awful. Then one day my manager said it wasn't working and I really needed to find a job somewhere else in the bank. I'd only been there 6 weeks – I knew no-one so there was no way I was going to be able to find another role. So I resigned."

Advice: Meet the team and the team manager in particular. Do they value what you're adding to the team? Do they understand and respect any parameters that you need to set? Are they prepared to support you? Do you have a sponsor at work who will help you deal with major issues if they arise?

4. Put your home team in place

Michelle's partner was surprised when she gave up a part time role near home to look for a more demanding job that involved a commute. Had she not taken time to explain her motivation, discuss how they all would make changes and get him on board, her return would have been impossible. As it was, when she secured her dream role he went part time for a while so that they could manage the transition together.

Advice: Be clear how your return will affect anyone impacted. It could be your partner, your friends, colleagues elsewhere, friends. Identify what support you will need, ask for it and think about what you can give in return. Of course, like just about everything, there's tech designed to help. Trello for example has some excellent family inspiration boards – you can all input, plan and track exactly what needs doing in a fun, simple, transparent way.

5. Ensure the sacrifices are worth it – financially and emotionally

When **Sharma** returned to work in fashion marketing, the thorn in her side was that her tasks were far more menial than previously, working for less prestigious clients. Her female bosses had had their children and returned to work almost immediately. Somewhat inevitably they had little empathy with women who wanted a degree of flexibility. As Sharma did. These employers were firmly of the "I took six weeks off, rolled my sleeves up and was back, cracking on from dawn to dust" school. Sharma hit a wall

"To be honest, I just wasn't prepared to doff my cap and scrape and bow just to be allowed to go to my son's nativity. I knew it was going to be hard, but I handed in my notice and decided to work for myself."

Advice: Understand what you're going to have to give up compared to your ideal role. Is it a title? Or a salary level? Or level of responsibility or access to certain clients or contacts? How does this compare to the sacrifices you're going to have to make at home and the effort you're going to have to put in place to make it work. It's a judgement call but is it worth it? If not, can you negotiate more?

6. Your new role is just that – new

Whether it's what you are paid, your status, your level of influence, your impact – you might need to accept that your new role will be different.

Lucy was a high performing marketing and brand manager in a Financial Services organisation. She wanted to go back when her daughter was 2 but rejected the idea of returning to a similar role.

"I would have just found it too frustrating. I needed to

work part time and there is no way I could have operated at the same level. I didn't want to suddenly feel mediocre, so I decided to find a role where I could deliver really high standards but in a part time capacity."

She is now working 2 ½ days a week for the British Chambers of Commerce: they love her because she is bringing much needed expertise to their team. They're happy, she's proud.

Advice: Don't judge yourself necessarily on your pre-break self. You may have more limitations on where you can spend your time. Work out what's really important to you, define your measures of success and find a role that fits.

7. Don't give up too quickly

Judith, who returned to Virgin Money, found being part of a cohort essential, as was having access to a coach.

"There were always times when one of us thought it was just too difficult. At one point I looked at the people working for me and thought I was in the wrong place – they had so many more years there than I did. But the other women in the group helped remind me of all the years of experience I'd had before my break. Having a coach work along-side us also really helped."

Advice: Set targets for yourself that are achievable. Recognise this is a transition and during that period you might need extra support. Have you agreed an onboarding process with your employer? Set up regular review and feedback meetings to discuss progress and agree any changes. Ask for a mentor and/or a buddy who can help.

8. Set your own bar

Think about what success looks like for you. Define it on your terms. Beware the danger of letting others do this for you.

Alex took 6 months paternity leave from his job as a management consultant. A high flier with an exemplary record of promotions and excellent performance reviews, he was confident that taking a break would not impact his career prospects. At the same time, seeing peers progress whilst he was on leave was a challenge. And he is still happy with his decision to take that time off. Not only would he do the same again, as a team manager he will be an advocate for promoting balance at work for parents of both genders. We need more leaders like him.

David, whose story follows below, is very clear, that you need to "manage your identity carefully" – recognise that work is just one element and that your identity as a father, a friend, a carer, is equally as important.

Advice: Taking a break from your career gives you a sense of perspective. You return changed. Your experience may have made you reevaluate what's important to you. Keep hold of that as you redefine what success looks like for you. Don't be bound by other people's definition of success. Their careers are their careers.

STRATEGIES AND TACTICS FOR ENSURING SUCCESS

A Checklist

Some aspects of your return will be unpredictable. You might find some things are much easier than you expected whilst some of the things you thought would be a breeze turn out to be much more problematic.

The purpose of the checklist below is to help you think through all of the various factors that could impact the success of your return. Are they relevant to you? Have you thought about them and have you taken some action if needed?

PREPARING YOURSELF

Success factor	Relevant Y/N	Done Y/N
I have clarity on what's most important to me about the role		
I am clear exactly what my parameters are around time – both in the office and working at home		
I know what my "red lines" are around all aspects of my role – seniority, title, responsibilities		
I am clear on the detail of what I will need to do to get the job done		
I know where any skills gaps are, and I have discussed where and how to access appropriate support or training		
I am clear on whether this is a stepping stone for me or my dream role		

	Relevant Y/N	Done Y/N
If it all works out, it feels like it will be worth it		
Where there are aspects of my role or terms of employment that I'm not happy about I have either negotiated or I have a plan to negotiate the necessary changes		

PREPARING THE HOME TEAM

Success factor	Relevant Y/N	Done Y/N
My partner (if you have one) understands and is supportive		
We have agreed contingency plans to deal with (insert detail ... Cancelled trains, meetings running late, children being ill...)		
I am clear what tasks I currently undertake that will need to be done some other way or by someone else		
We have discussed as a family what my return means for everyone and everyone understands this		
I have communicated with other people who are affected, and they know how to help		
We have a three to six month plan that recognises that period might be tricky		

PREPARATION AT WORK

Success factor	Relevant Y/N	Done Y/N
I have a clear sponsor in the organisation		
There is an agreed onboarding process for my first week, month, three months		
We have discussed any skills or knowledge gaps and there is a plan in place to help me close them		

My immediate team and line manager knows what I'm bringing to the organisation and how I will be working		
My immediate team and line manager is supportive of the parameters around my working day/week		
I know how I'm going to be measured and who is doing the measuring		
I am clear on my responsibilities in terms of managing and developing others		
I understand potential development opportunities and future career path options		

THE EMOTIONAL JOURNEY

Deciding you're sufficiently motivated to want to return to work or step up your career is a significant life change. It's an emotional journey as well as a practical one.

This section uses a tool to set out why it can feel you're in the middle of a maelstrom. It's based on the work of William Bridges and outlined in his book *Managing Transitions*.

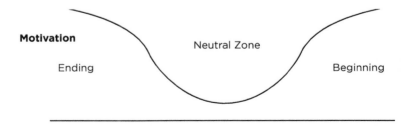

Bridges writes about there being three phases to any change: endings; a neutral zone; and new beginnings. When organisations make changes there is a clear 'endings' phase; a 'neutral zone' when some people are still hanging on to the old and others are actively preparing for the new; and finally a 'beginning' phase when the new way of working has set in.

For women returning after a career break each phase brings with it different emotions. This model can help explain what you might be experiencing – both positive and negative. Acknowledging, understanding and even expecting these feelings can be a great help.

Ending: What's ending? How you feel will probably be influenced by how far you are making a return through choice or through necessity.

Some endings might feel positive: boredom, a sense of being unfulfilled, too much time on your hands, having to do the school run every day.

There are other endings could feel more like losses. The time spent with children, if you have them. Freedom and time for yourself. The ability to take on other responsibilities, volunteering roles, hobbies, sports. A loss of autonomy as you take on a role working for someone else.

Neutral Zone: This middle phase of the transitions process can be the most turbulent of all.

One you decide you want to return or be promoted, you will be impatient to get started and may feel very frustrated when it doesn't happen quickly. If your CV or job application is rejected time after time, it can become quite disheartening, depressing even.

It can be a time of great uncertainty and ambiguity. You want to work but you're not sure how to get back. You want to change careers but are not clear which of your transferable skills will be most relevant. Work has changed since you left, will it even be possible to go back. Should you get a job or work for yourself?

It can be tempting to jump at the first job that's offered, to move out of an unsettled period. It's a job, it's money. That's not always the right thing to do. Sometimes, even after you've accepted a role and are back working, it can feel as though you stuck in the middle – in that neutral or "transition" zone – trying to be a partner, parent and a model employee.

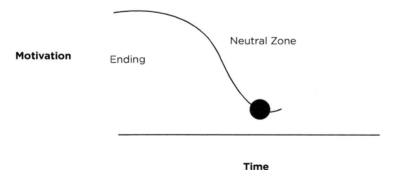

New Beginnings: Beginnings are a phase not a point in time. How long does it take to feel comfortable and confident in a new job?

In Abi's story, above, her found job at the online magazine

As a management consultant, David is used to creating solutions, fixing things and empowering people to change. But home life showed that there aren't always solutions, and you can't convince people to change. So he spent more time understanding, learning, accepting, challenging, supporting and being supported.

It also gave him the opportunity to reflect on the shape and direction of his family's life. He learnt to be patient, never to give up. Caring for his disabled child was incredibly rewarding, seeing his progress, little by little and enjoying small surprises. It can also be brutal and lonely – the intensity of care leaves little room for much else, physically or mentally.

He learned to cope better, to be kinder to himself, to recognise, in his words "that you're not tarnished or weakened, rather you're stronger, with more skills and experience that are relevant to professional roles too. My time away gave me better perspective. Work doesn't define me as much. The space gave me time to reflect on what I like, who I like and what's important to me. I'm clearer now about what I want to do and how much of myself I will give to work. My boundaries are clearer, but with the right people and in the right environment I think I will actually add more value."

David is now back at work and returns changed. Not just as an individual but also as a leader.

"I realise that our energies have to be managed more carefully. We all have lots of things going on in our lives.

We need to give people time and space – if you squeeze them too much that's just wrong. We need to be much more flexible in how we define roles, agree ways of working and set incentives."

WHAT ASTRONAUTS CAN TEACH US ABOUT RETURNING TO WORK

As any astronaut will tell you, launching into space is the easy part. The difficult bit is re-entry. Returning to earth is much trickier. So much can go wrong.

Leaving a job whilst emotionally difficult, is actually relatively straightforward from a practical perspective. The same cannot be said of a return to work. So, what are the lessons from space travel?

1. **Atmospheric entry can either be uncontrolled** – meteors falling to earth, for example – or **controlled**, such as the re-entry of a spacecraft, capable of being navigated and supported in its journey. No prizes for guessing which one of these is more successful.

   When you are returning after a career break, you need a plan and you need support. You've been operating in a different atmosphere. With a different schedule, different rules and a different measure of what success looks like. Like any good plan it needs to be funded, time-bound, with specific actions and clarity around the support you are going to need.

2. **Astronauts have to navigate the right path back to earth.**

Spaceships can't just pick any route home. Space is full of all sorts of dangerous objects and potential barriers. When you are thinking about returning to work after a career break, the route back is often not straightforward either. You may need flexibility, which the employer you left is not prepared to offer. You may actually want a change of direction, building on skills and experience gained in your break.

What will help your journey back? Word of mouth and contacts. So, navigate your way back by being clear about what you want, what you excel at and the value you can add. And work those contacts.

3. **A spaceship has to re-enter the earth at a certain angle or it will bounce into space and never be seen again.**

Spaceships slow down significantly from their extreme orbit speed as they prepare for re-entry. They also have to adopt a different position as they descend through the atmosphere. They change shape, it takes time.

When you have been a full-time carer, even if you have also been doing voluntary work or running your own business, a transition back to the workplace takes preparation and time.

The things you were doing at home are not going to go away. So who is going to step up and help? It could be about getting more domestic help, it could be about your children or partner stepping up. Just make sure you don't bounce back simply because your new workload is just not manageable.

4. Astronauts are supported by a huge team on the ground.

Many companies say they are keen to hire more experienced women. So how do you figure out which ones really mean it? The ones that are prepared to support you. Who recognise that this is a transition and that you may need some support. Not just with the technical training involved but also in navigating the politics, networks and the 'unwritten rules' around how things work.

Just as importantly, though, the team on the ground at NASA recognise that the astronaut is returning with some immensely valuable skills and experience. Skills and experience that they could not have gathered in their labs. Is this true of the company you are about to join? Do they value the different perspective you bring?

5. It takes time for Astronauts to readjust to earth.

Astronauts returning from the International Space Station have to go through a 45-day reconditioning programme.

That's why smart organisations offer tailored training and coaching programmes for people returning after a significant career break.

The message for anyone returning? Give yourself time and make sure you identify exactly what training and support you need. It might be a coach but equally it could be finding a young mentor who would also benefit from learning from your wisdom and experience.

Your Checklist for the Chapter

✓ Are you realistic about what you can handle at the moment?

✓ Do you understand fully what's expected of you in the role – and the level of support you can expect in return?

✓ Are the people around you in your new role clear on your commitment., your skills, your availability?

✓ Can you find a sponsor or mentor to help you with the bumpy first few months?

✓ Have you told the people at home how this will affect them – and how they can help?

✓ Have you worked out realistic measures of success that mean something to you – and a sensible time frame to achieve this?

Other Resources

Managing Transitions: Making the most of change by William Bridges

What's going on inside when change happens? What's the emotional impact and how do you minimise disruption.

Half a Wife: The Working Family's Guide to Getting a Life Back by Gaby Hinsliff

Mothers Work! How to get a grip on guild and make a smooth return to work by Jessica Chivers

SECTION THREE

1.

If not now, when?

When we mooted the idea of writing this book, people told us it was "too niche". Yet it has never felt more like the right time to be writing about women taking their seat at the table.

Looking at what's going on around us, it feels as though we are entering a period of tectonic change in the world of work. Some changes are driven by the digital revolution, which may still prove to be in its infancy; others by a shifting focus around the world to concerns about sustainability; others by a sharpening of the political focus around fairness and equality. Many of these macro trends suggest to us that now is the time.

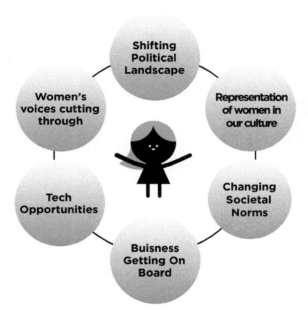

THE POLITICAL LANDSCAPE IS CHANGING

"There's an awareness of issues that were previously unspoken or unseen. It's the government's role to create a hospitable environment for businesses to thrive and ensure there is level playing field for everyone – including women."

Sarah Wood, CEO and Founder, Unruly

2018 was the centenary of women in the UK first securing the right to vote. The London Mayor, Sadiq Khan, launched a major campaign #BehindEveryGreatCity, which champions the achievements and contributions of women, from all walks of life, that make cities great.

The campaign followed research which found that, in London, three times more women than men say that their gender hinders their progression at work. With support from business leaders like Sarah, it encourages Londoners – individuals, organisations and institutions – to make a commitment to take actions which will make a difference.

Campaigns like this are powerful, but changes to legislation are even more so. In the UK, the introduction of Gender Pay Gap reporting has forced a country-wide conversation about pay inequalities in several walks of life.

And to quote Dame Helena Morrissey in a recent Sunday Times interview:

"It won't be a good enough excuse to say, 'Oh it's because we don't have many senior women' – because that's the whole point!"

These conversations are leading to further questions about how to enable more women to get through to those senior positions and how to ensure equality for women at *all* levels, across all organisations.

WOMEN'S VOICES ARE CUTTING THROUGH

Women have had enough of being underpaid, harassed, undervalued, underemployed, unseen and unheard. And our voices, more than ever, are being heard.

The ability to connect through social media has removed traditional gatekeepers from the mainstream media which in turn has enabled campaigns like #MeToo and #TimesUp to gather global momentum as never before. The images shared from events such as the Women's March create momentum and demonstrate strength in numbers.

Women are giving voice to their experiences and to demand and enable change.

OUR STORIES ARE BEING SHARED

In the past, the stories we saw on TV, in film and in the media were shaped predominantly by men. This is changing as more women step in.

Sharon Horgan – writer and actress – is now a significant global industry player aged 47, co-founding her own production company Merman. She talked recently about why it's so important to have more women commissioning, writing, producing and directing.

> **"**It's a boy's club, there's no denying that, and that's why we still need these programmes that champion women, give them a safe space to work in, to change that narrative entirely.**"** Sharon Horgan

Action from women like Sharon, Reese Witherspoon, Elizabeth Moss, Greta Gerwig, Ava Duvernay and others has seen in increase in highly successful, revenue generating, award winning stories led by women.

There's a swathe of film and theatre producers and directors scooping up awards and attracting audiences in their millions. Their stories feature women as leads with a narrative that is firmly female-driven.

Seeing, hearing and sharing more of our stories is shaping our culture in a way that's exciting and tremendously encouraging. This is critical because stories are at the heart of our culture. They are how we process the world. The more we hear and share those stories, the better for all of us.

BUSINESSES UNDERSTAND THAT PEOPLE WANT SOMETHING DIFFERENT

Businesses recognise that they need more diversity if they are to succeed in a world that will demand ever increasing creativity and innovation. And that's not just about gender. The most far-sighted also recognise that they need to change if they are to attract a generation of people who are not prepared to sign up to 80-hour weeks and who are not looking for jobs for life.

Agile working at Deloitte

When Emma Codd took on the role of Talent Partner for Deloitte in 2013, she had two priorities. Flexibility and gender.

"They were linked," she told us, "but they were not the

same thing. Everything we read, all the evidence was telling us that millennials wanted more out of their lives. We knew we needed to change the culture of long hours and presenteeism. For everyone."

The first thing Emma did was ditch the word Flexibility, which had become jaded, and replace it with Agile, with a set of new policies aimed at both men and women.

One of the most innovative was the introduction of Time Out. Anyone out of a training contract could apply to take an extra month off, unpaid, at a time to suit them and the business. Every year. And the month could be tacked onto holiday.

Take up was slow. Despite visible commitment from the CEO, David, and an impressive internal comms campaign, people were concerned that taking up the offer would impact their career. They needed to see it and believe it. Emma and David focused their efforts on building commitment amongst the partnership, encouraging leaders to get involved. This included measuring take up levels in different parts of the business and calling out any leaders who were clearly not supportive. It worked.

Over 900 people have taken advantage of Time Out since it was introduced, split evenly between men and women. Everyone comes back from their breaks visibly refreshed and re-energised.

It works because it is underpinned by 3 principles: Trust and respect; open and honest communication; and judging only on output.

TECHNOLOGY IS TRANSFORMING THE WORLD OF WORK

The digital revolution has transformed our lives as consumers; and it feels as though the world of work is also beginning to transform.

Technology is redefining where work happens, who does it, when and at what cost. Tools such as Slack, Google Docs, Google Hangouts, Trello and Dropbox all facilitate agile working, reducing the need to be in a swanky, expensive office 5 days a week. Companies are reducing their footprint – they have fewer desks available – so staff needs are more fluid, open to negotiation and less dependent on everyone being present at the same time every day of the week.

We can now collaborate with anyone, anywhere, with a few taps on a phone. It's the future – and it's here.

New business models are springing up, challenging the status quo. They are doing things differently, developing fresh, often audacious challenger business models. They've observed there is an extraordinary talent pool whose life demands no longer fit a traditional working model.

One of these is **PowerToFly** – who use proprietary search and sourcing tools to connect companies with underrepresented female engineers at a lower cost. Their engineers are based all over the world – because when you code, or develop, where you do this isn't really the critical factor.

For women with an entrepreneurial bent, it's easier than ever to set up your own business and get your product or services to market. The giants of the digital economy provide great opportunities for your new venture. They are democratising business, giving the small start-up access to the same tools, capabilities and reach as the big corporates.

Millions of small challenger brands advertise on Google and Facebook to reach their customers. New startups unlock the power of Amazon and Shopify to create digital shop windows for their products – giving them access to customers all around the world. These platforms handle the charging of the products and even the logistics of distribution.

SOCIETAL NORMS

New conversations about masculinity and mental health mean that men, as well as women, are starting to think about how they balance work and a personal life. Fewer people want to be chained to their desks all week every week for every year of their working lives. People quite rightly, are seeking a rich, fulfilling life outside of work. And too right, given how long we're all going to be working.

A career that can adapt, change, grow throughout your working life. The possibility of being involved in parenting your child without throwing the towel in on your career. A mid-life career change. Taking time off to look after your elderly parents. Or to pursue a creative dream. Or to travel. Work that is fulfilling and stimulating and which also leaves you space and time to fulfil your personal ambitions. What's not to like?

As Andy Woodfield, partner at PwC put it succinctly to us:

"Men want this shit too."

OVER TO YOU

Change is afoot. And at the same time, women can't wait for institutions and organisations to take action. The time is right for you to pick up the baton. Be brave. Be ambitious for yourself and your future career.

> **"I believe ambition is not a dirty word. Ambition is simply a drive inside of you – it's having a curiosity or a new idea and the desire to pursue it."**
> Reese Witherspoon

Why end this call to action with a quote from a wealthy, successful, privileged actress? Because Reese Witherspoon saw a problem – a lack of decent roles for women in a male-dominated film industry – and did something about it. She established her own production company and went on to capitalize on the demand for women's stories, telling them in every single medium: TV, film, and online.

And we're all about action.

We're encouraging that same ambition for you. Why? There's NEVER been a better time.

2.

Other resources

Articles

Here are some of the articles we find ourselves returning to again and again.

Reassessing the Gender Wage Gap by Marina N. Bolotnikova, Harvard Magazine May-June 2016.

Why Women Still Can't Have it All by Anne-Marie Slaughter in The Atlantic, July/August 2012.

Mind the Gap and Close It by Ellevest, available on Ellevest. com.

Why Diversity Programs Fail by Frank Dobbin and Alexandra Kalev.

Podcasts

Our new favourite way to stimulate our thinking. Unlike reading, can be done whilst walking the dog.

Eat Sleep Work Repeat A podcast about happiness and work culture, hosted by Bruce Daisley, European VP for Twitter.

The Broad Experience a conversation about women, the workplace and success, hosted by Ashley Milne-Tyte.

Freakonomics Radio conversations exploring the riddles of everyday life, including lots on the gender pay gap and women's careers, hosted by Stephen J. Dubner.

Fortunately with Fi and Jane smart women having interesting conversations to put a spring in your step, hosted by Jane Garvey and Fi Glover.

HBR: *Women at Work* Conversations about the workplace and women's place in it.

Fiction

Where to start? We could go on and on but as we're tipping into self-indulgence territory and possibly trying your patience, here are 10 books we love. They all feature inspirational, thoughtful or extraordinary female protagonists.

The Handmaid's Tale by Margaret Atwood

The Dept of Speculation by Jenny Offill

I Know Why the Caged Bird Sings by Maya Angelou

Heartburn by Nora Ephron

Gone with the Wind by Margaret Mitchell

Americanah by Chimamanda Ngozi Adichie

Beloved by Toni Morrison

Pride and Prejudice by Jane Austen

Anne of Green Gables by L.M. Montgomery

What Katy Did by Susan Coolidge.

Non-Fiction

Stepping Up: How to accelerate your leadership potential by Sarah Wood

What's Mine is Yours: How collaborative consumption is changing the way we live by Rachel Botsam and Roo Rogers

A Good Time to be a Girl by Helena Morrissey

What I know for sure by Oprah Winfrey
Because it's OPRAH! The only time we have used an exclamation mark in this book. Oh yes.

Drive: the surprising truth about what motivates us by Dan Pink
What really makes us tick – autonomy, mastery, purpose.

We should all be feminists by Chimamanda Ngozi Adichie
Nuff said.

How to be a Woman by Caitlin Moran
Witty, astute and packed full of sage advice.

Half a Wife by Gaby Hinsliff
A practical guide for guilt torn parents. Mothers and fathers.

The Descent of Man by Grayson Perry
What makes a man? Is it time to redefine masculinity? We do hope so.

Goodnight Stories for Rebel Girls by Elena Favilli and Francesca Cavallo
Stories of amazing women to share with your children.
Not a princess or a frog in sight (and a % of profits goes to providing more girls with access to education).

Little Black Book: A toolkit for working women by Otegha Uwagba
Fresh ideas, creative insights – practical, fun and small enough to fit in your handbag.

It's Not How Good you Are it's how Good you want to Be by Paul Arden
Ideas from the world of advertising that translate niftily into lessons in life.

Bossypants by Tina Fey
Feminism, body image, making it in a man's world and women being very, very funny.

Bedsit Disco Queen: How I grew up and tried to be a pop star by Tracey Thorn
Part memoir of a long career, motherhood and studying, part manifesto of a woman achieving in the pop industry – poignant, insightful lyrics about the different stages of women's lives.

#Girlboss by Sophia Amoruso
Frank observations from the founder of Nasty Gal.

Linchpin: Are You Indispensable? How to drive your career and create a remarkable future by Seth Godin
Modern career advice from one of the smartest thinkers around.

10 Rules for Success by Karren Brady
Practical tips for women in business.

Women & Power: A Manifesto by Mary Beard
A witty take on gender agenda and how history has treated powerful women.

3.

The story of how we wrote this book

You've made it this far. Thank you. The last thing we'd like to do is leave you with the story of how we wrote this book. Why? Because, much like finding well paid work, it was tough.

Half way through the process we sat down with our friend Ruth, a PR specialist, bemoaning just how difficult it was and describing how we were amassing a team of test readers. She laughed and said:

"You should write the story of how you wrote the book."

So here it is.

What made us want to write a book in the first place? Well, to begin with we like to think we're pretty good at writing. At creating clear, compelling, jargon free comms that tell it like it is. And we believed that a book was needed. A practical handbook to let women know they are not mad – that the world of work IS NOT currently designed to help them have both a career and a family. A guide which would explain what they can do about it.

Everyone told us the first step to getting a book published was to find an agent.

Our writer friend Matthew introduced us to his highly respected agent who was very helpful but our book (short, action packed, humorous, we hope) was not really her thing (historical, long, extremely well researched, erudite). A different Matthew (do keep up, there's another due to come along any minute) introduced us to a more glitzy talent agency and there we signed with an enthusiastic agent.

We waited for the publishing contract to roll in. It did. But for a 70,000 word business book with no colour, no pictures and no diagrams. And since no woman we know has the time to sit down and read a 70,000 word business book, our handy little handbook remained unpublished.

Our agent moved on to other, more promising ventures. At least he tried.

We approached other agents. Women who completely empathised with where we were coming from. Who had plenty of friends and acquaintances who would benefit from the advice we were proposing to offer. Would they represent us? No.

Why not?

"It's too niche."

"It's a bit like that other book, just published." (it wasn't)

"We've not had much success with career books for women."

"You're not famous enough."

One told us that if we have thousands of followers on Instagram we might just find an agent. Another suggested that we make the book gender neutral.

We listened graciously to all the advice they offered. And ignored it.

We thought about self-publishing but that didn't feel right for us – we're not great completer/finishers for a start. Someone not called Matthew introduced us to Unbound (which funnily enough is run by someone called Mathew with one t). Unbound is a highly successful, business model where you use all the traditional publishing channels but pre-sell through crowdsourcing.

Unbound were keen to work with us. Hurrah. At last. Then... we explored the model in a little more detail. As we understood it, it would be up to us (the unfamous ones, pushing a niche book for an audience that allegedly doesn't want it) to raise all the funding to get the book to market. Oh, and it would be published in 18 months' time.

So, we'd have to spend three months cajoling everyone we know to buy in advance. At this point we had about 13,000 words written. More of a booklet. Or a glorified pamphlet. We had a choice. Spend time raising money to publish a book that currently wasn't written or spend time writing the thing.

Turns out chapter 3 is spot on. It's not what you know, it's who you know. Our client Nigel Slater, head of consulting at KPMG, introduced us to the smart and kind Stephen Frost who has his own Diversity & Inclusion consultancy, Frost Included. Stephen had published a couple of books and made an introduction for us to Matthew Smith (told you there was another one coming along), founder and publishing director of Urbane Publications.

Matthew had years of publishing experience behind him and knew that world inside out. We met over coffee. He got us. He got the book. Immediately. We explained that of course our book needed colour, the odd diagram and was certainly nowhere near 70,000 words.

"How many?" He asked.

"More like 20,000. Or maybe 25,000."

"That's not a book that's a pamphlet," he said. "If your book is going to deliver what you say it is, it's going to have to be around 45,000 words. If not, it can't possibly have the insights you say it will and the reviewers will tear it apart."

Say what you like about Matthew number 3, but he doesn't mince his words.

Luckily, he didn't ditch us as flakey wannabe writers there and then and we agreed to go and rethink how much material we had, realistically.

We cut and pasted everything we had ever written – magazine articles, newspaper commentary, Linkedin articles, our own newsletters – shoved it all in on document and did a word count. 20,000 words. Halfway there.

Deb suggested we try to visualise the book. Lisa resisted. Then did this exercise and loved it. That's how we roll.

The only way we could get our heads around the task was to break it down into bite sized pieces. We brainstormed all the individual chapters and talked about what would go in each one. 12 lots of 3,500 feels a lot more manageable than 45,000 words somehow.

Matthew came on board and said he'd love to work with us. He was enthusiastic, direct, positive and even more pushy than us.

"We'll need to publish at the end of May. The manuscript has to be done and dusted by the end of February. I'll sort out the

ISBN number, you need to agree on the title and subtitle soon. Cover needs to be finished before Christmas." It was October.

We had a publisher, the beginnings of a book, and a small but growing following in our Facebook group. We were still not famous, though.

Lisa had met Arianna Huffington over the summer. Lisa had agreed to do some writing for Thrive Global, Arianna's new organisation, where the team had decided to launch a section on the website specifically on the subject of Women in the Workplace. Arianna was acutely aware of the leaky pipeline of female talent, which is as much of a problem in the US as it is in the UK.

We approached Arianna to ask if she'd endorse the book.

"Of course, send me the manuscript," she replied. Sometimes it pays to build a relationship with a famous, inspirational and extremely action focused woman.

Now all we had to do was write the thing. Which we did. Chapter by chapter. Word by word. Pretty much every single paragraph of our original 20,000 has been chopped, changed, or deleted. They say all writing is rewriting. That's certainly our experience.

We began thinking about how to sell the book. We ran our ideas by Matthew early in December, suggesting that we reach out to a couple of journalists we knew now to let them know what was coming. He reined us in.

"We don't want to do anything that's going to look half-arsed and slipshod," were his exact words.

Ashley, Lisa's husband and a very good salesman, had the answer.

"Stop worrying about selling, make sure you write the best book ever."

So that was us told. Nothing half-arsed and slipshod. Only the best will do.

As we approached something that looked like half a book, we began to get cold feet. What if it was no good? What if no-one would read it?

Deb got talking to someone at the News UK Start Up lab, who suggested that like all good inventions, we should put out a prototype and test it. So we appealed to our Facebook group for test readers, got some volunteers and, with a great deal of trepidation, sent them our first three chapters to read.

(Apparently test readers are a big thing amongst cookery writers, who use them to test recipes. We can thoroughly recommend them).

Our test readers gave us amazing insights and detailed feedback, but the most important thing they gave us was the confidence and enthusiasm to continue. They wrote things like:

"I've just read through this and will take the time to feedback thoroughly but thought an articulation of my initial thoughts would be helpful...HELL YEAH!"

"Overall I found it open, human and engaging – and it made me smile too."

"I enjoyed reading this – it looks to me like it will be a good addition to the thinking on this topic. I'd definitely like to read the rest of the book."

"Loved this! Particularly your style – felt like you were talking to me. Very easy/quick read which is helpful for busy mothers. Felt practical and thought provoking and just an enjoyable read."

"I can't stand self-help books (which is why I haven't read any and maybe why I'm stuck). But I like this one. Please can you hurry up and write the rest of it!"

We began to socialise some of the content and messaging with our Facebook group and on LinkedIn, mobilising the power of our online network. We reached out to all the experts we had met over the years, to ask if they would help with their own specialist area of content. To a woman (and man) they all said yes.

It soon felt as though we had a proverbial tribe of women – and men – who had our back. Our vision for what the book needed to look like was taking shape. We found women and men who were willing to tell us their stories, we read articles and books, watched YouTube videos, walked the dog listening to podcasts.

With a clear vision of the stories we wanted to tell, armed with the strategies, tactics and advice that we believed was relevant and useful and with support from the famous – Arianna Huffington and Sarah Wood in particular – and the not so famous but just as fabulous, we pressed on and gradually our book came to life.

It has colour, pictures and diagrams. Everything we dreamed of. And most surprising of all, at the last count it was just shy of 60,000 words long.

And if you've stayed with us this far, thank you.

INDEX

ACKNOWLEDGEMENTS

We have to start by saying thank you to our husbands Ashley and Simon. Not only did Ash sacrifice the use of his home office, he also took on the mantle of head salesman, constantly telling anyone he met how brilliant the book was. Simon was our technical go to, a font of all knowledge about the way the world is changing and a dab hand in superb one liners.

Our children – Florence, Luca, Ethan and Isaac – are firmly front and centre of Team She's Back. They worked at our events (we had no one else), edited our website (we were hopeless), posted on their social feeds (they're Gen X, they know this way better than us). They're engaged and relentlessly enthusiastic.

Their practical support and encouragement means the world.

Arianna Huffington, Sarah Wood and Matthew d'Ancona made a huge difference to us. We are (still) not famous and our Instagram account is woeful. By showing their faith in us and endorsing the book they helped us overcome those hurdles. They made others sit up and take notice.

Thank you to the many other Matthews involved, particularly Matthew Smith our publisher, who took a punt on us. And made sure that nothing was "half-arsed and slipshod". We hope.

Lots of people read different pieces of the book for us, but our tireless team of test readers:

Victoria Knox, Nicola Fomes, Uzma Mohamedali, Jo Cochrane, Katy Whelan, Zoe Warren and Georgina Creighton went above and beyond the call of duty. We almost don't care what the reviewers say, these are all intelligent, thoughtful women and they thought it was fab, which is more than good enough for us.

Thanks too for all the experts who contributed to individual chapters and made sure that the advice we're offering is sound: particularly Victoria McLean, Stephanie Dillon, Karen Mattison MBE, Julianne Miles, Dominie Moss, Michelle Gyimah.

This book would be nothing without the stories of the real people who to time share their experience, including Kay Hughes, David Lancefield, Melanie Eusebe, Rohati Chapman, Ann O'Neil, Jenni Veitch, Jane Price-Stephens, Marcus Wildsmith, Emma Pritchard, Alex Soutsos, Annoushka Ducas MBE, Ruth Cairns, Sally Day, Emma Niven, Jennifer Ross, Annalie Riches, Laura Fisher, Helen Philpott Jenny Cowderoy, Judith Bradbury, Michelle Thresh, Emma Codd, Emily Khan, Ruth Cherry and Lucy Froese.

Lisa Unwin is the founder of She's Back, a business whose purpose is to enable business to access the unique talent in women returning to work after an extended career break. A former partner with Arthur Andersen Business Consulting and Director of Brand and Communication at Deloitte, Lisa had a 20-year career in professional services prior to setting up She's Back.